Bill Harrison

Six Days on a Raft

Bill Harrison with Forrest Haggerty

Bloomington, IN  Milton Keynes, UK

authorHOUSE®

AuthorHouse™
1663 Liberty Drive, Suite 200
Bloomington, IN 47403
www.authorhouse.com
Phone: 1-800-839-8640

AuthorHouse™ UK Ltd.
500 Avebury Boulevard
Central Milton Keynes, MK9 2BE
www.authorhouse.co.uk
Phone: 08001974150

First published by AuthorHouse 2/8/2007

ISBN: 978-1-4259-8369-7 (sc)
ISBN: 978-1-4259-8368-0 (hc)

Printed in the United States of America
Bloomington, Indiana

This book is printed on acid-free paper.

Dedication

This book is dedicated to the memory of my comrades from the U.S.S. YMS – 472 who never made it home – Charles Griffith Bates Jr., Gerard Henry Bernard Jr., Captain Willard Blazer, Thomas William Boivin, Thaddeus Martin Cullinan Jr., Glendene Daugherty, John Roy Eaves Jr., Colie Blease Gilchrist, Donald Raymond Hartman, Edward Cecil Hicks, Robert Hobart, Albert Joseph Jones, Edward Joseph Koniar, Richard Edmond Lewis, Stanley Zacharus Marks, William Andy Martin Jr., Joseph Francis Mendello, Percy "J" Pavey, Norman Wolcott Plumb, Joseph Robert Quather, Henry Rieb, Charles Eurcel Sigfriet, Boyd Weaver Stauffer, Paul Joseph Termine Jr., and Donald Clyde Van Arman. You were never forgotten.

"Bill and I were two of many to heed our country's call to arms. He survived six days on a raft in the Pacific. I survived nine months in a German POW camp. We were the lucky ones. Always remember those who perished in our fight for freedom."

Richard T. Blomberg Jr.
Lt. Colonel USAF Ret.

Day One

CHAPTER I

"I made a promise to God while floating on a raft with nothing to eat or drink for six days, and after watching five of my buddies slip into the ocean. This promise was that if God would send help, and we were rescued, I would do all within my power to further the cause of faith in God and this is why I am writing this book."

—Bill Harrison

Our ship started to break up and go down around midnight September 16, 1945, one month after the close of W.W.II. Prior to this typhoon our job had been to sweep the waters off the coast of Okinawa and clear the area of any unexploded mines. On this particular day, September 16, 1945, we had been riding out the typhoon from six that morning. Just before I headed down to the engine room to start my four-hour duty I was in the wheelhouse, and I remember Edward Cecil Hicks, our Yeoman, was just completing his four-hour watch at the wheel. As the typhoon grew more intense the pitching and rolling grew more severe, and as Hicks was leaving the wheelhouse I remember him saying, "I am so seasick I am going down to the crews quarters and going to bed. I'll bolt the hatches behind me and if the ship goes down so be it. I am so sick I just don't care." That was the last time I ever saw Edward.

As for myself, I was too scared to be seasick. It was at this point that my instinct to survive kicked into high gear. A huge determination to stay alive overtook me. I wanted to deal with each roadblock as it came. When I went down into the engine room I wanted to stay alive more than ever. That was all I could really focus on while I was doing my job for the next four hours.

Busy, but concerned over the pitching and pounding the ship was taking in this violent storm, I performed my job, as always, to the best of my ability, and my shift ended right at midnight. For four hours I was deep in the ship's belly making sure our engines maintained their power while being bounced around continuously. Aware of the intensity of the typhoon in which we were caught, and even though tired and sleepy, the bottom of the ship's crew's quarters was not in my plans. I made the decision to go directly to the wheelhouse when I completed my shift. Being above the water line and with twelve of my shipmates, this seemed to me to be the safest spot on the ship in the middle of this raging storm.

The pounding had been taking its toll on our ship. We were heading directly into every wave rising up over the top of it, thus causing our ship to fall and slap the trough behind each wave as we came down the backside of it. It was wave after wave after wave. I had never seen so many giant waves concentrated into such a short time period in my whole life. Eventually the abuse from this pounding ride split the weld seams that held the fuel tank together for the electrical generator. When the seams split it did not take long for all the fuel to leak out of the tanks. It was only a matter of a minute or two. When that happened we lost all electrical power as well as our power steering. We were not dead in the water because our engine was still running, but we were unable to steer the ship directly into the waves as easily as before. The helmsman could no longer steer by himself. The force of the water pushing against the rudder was too great for him to handle alone. He had to have somebody help him. We ended up with two men at the wheel using all their might just to try and keep the ship straight. They had one heck of a time. With all the power out we could not even radio for help. I knew it was only a matter of time before our ship broached. That is, it was only a matter of time before our ship became parallel to the waves. A broached ship in the middle of a typhoon is a sailor's worst nightmare. All we could do at this point is sit and hope that our ship would be able to withstand all the abuse it had endured and all the abuse that lie ahead. I knew it was not going to be long before our ship would be in grave danger if the storm did not start letting up, and if we did not have some form of help coming our way we too would be in the same situation as our ship.

I went below deck and began telling my shipmates what was happening. I let them know about our unfortunate situation and how we were struggling to steer our ship directly into the giant waves. Those who were below deck I was telling to go topside. Afterwards, I went topside and waited to see what fate had in store for us.

It was about fifteen minutes after I finished with my work in the engine room when I came back to the wheelhouse. The two sailors at the wheel were still fighting to keep the ship going straight into the waves. Our ship would slightly broach and the two would strain to true her course. We were still without electrical power, so all we could do is just sit and wait in the glow of the dim red light that was illuminating from the magnetic compass. Without the power steering the ship kept turning in such a way that it was taking on the waves from the side. First it would hit our port side, then we would turn and get hit on the starboard side. It was after a wave hit our starboard side that the two struggling helmsmen trued the ship back into the waves, however the force of the water and wind tended to cause the ship to over correct. We were slightly broached with the next wave getting ready to strike our port side as I sat down on a metal toolbox that was inside the wheelhouse. At this point I heard the most odd meow from our cat we had as a mascot. The cat seemed to know something the rest of us did not know. He was on deck just outside one of the windows. As I started to make my way to let the cat in, the ship, suddenly and viciously, began tumbling. Instantly everything went black as water poured into the cabin. I could hear the breaking of glass mixed in with screaming and yelling that turned into gargling water. Many of my shipmates were inhaling seawater and beginning to drown in the panic of this cataclysmic event. I never knew men could scream such a guttural yell. It seemed to come from the most primitive instinct to survive. These screams of terror were as scary as the horrifying state of affairs I found myself in. At first I thought it was just a bad dream, but a bigger part of me knew it was sickeningly real. Everything seemed to move in slow motion at this point. Part of me could not believe it was really happening while another part of me instinctually struggled to stay alive. Bodies were tumbling everywhere. Guys were falling on me, stepping on me and equipment was being tossed in all directions. What actually only lasted maybe twenty seconds seemed to take forever. Those were some of the longest seconds in my life.

After the tumbling came to a stop, I found myself under water tangled up with a web of bodies and the metal toolbox on my chest. I pushed the metal toolbox off of me and fought my way through the twisted mess of panicking bodies that were my shipmates. I stood up. Fortunately my head rose above the water line. Immediately, and rapidly, I could feel the water rising on my body. My first thought was, 'the ship is going down.' My second thought was, 'I need to breathe as long as possible,' so I started to move and feel in total darkness amidst rising water, and the nonstop guttural cries for help. In this sheer darkness and total chaos, it was every man for himself. It was impossible to try and help someone else when I was not even sure how to help myself. At this point my body was on automatic and it was running on pure adrenaline and a strong impulse to live. I headed in a direction where there was nothing blocking my path. I was stopped when I reached a partition, which later I determined to be the ceiling of the wheelhouse. In the motion of feeling around, I found something familiar to me. It was an electrical cable that ran along the ceiling of the cabin. Wedging my fingers behind the cable I lifted my self out of the water until my head slammed into another partition. For what seemed like an eternity, I hung to the cable for a short while realizing I would be able to breathe a little longer. After a few seconds had passed I felt the wind start to blow in on the left side of my face. I knew that was my

3

passage to freedom, and as strange as it was, under these dire circumstances I had a feeling of euphoria knowing I had a way out, because it was not going to be much longer before the confined space of the wheelhouse would become my tomb. Reaching for the ribs of the ship, hand over hand I pulled myself toward this incoming wind. As I grew closer, I could see the dim outline of the sky through the hatchway from which the wind blew. Ironically, that immediately put me in a very happy state of mind. At least I knew I was not going to die inside the ship's wheelhouse.

As I made my way to the opening, one of my shipmates began crawling out ahead of me. Given the lighting conditions at the time it was impossible to tell who it was. As I began to crawl out myself I felt another one of my shipmates grab at my legs and feet. As I was crawling through the portal, I caught my bearings and could tell that the back half of the ship was below the surface while it was resting on its side, and the front half was pointing up at about a thirty-degree angle. At this point two thoughts entered my mind. The first thought was, 'I needed to get off the hull.' The second thought was, 'I needed to get as far away from the ship as possible.' I had no desire to be pulled down by the ship's powerful suction when it went under. At that same moment I realized I had enough time to get to the nearest life raft. Crawling on my hands and knees, I made my way to the raft. Upon my arrival I could see there were already two of my shipmates there trying to release it. The three of us struggled to release the latches to no avail. They were frozen shut from salt-water corrosion. We could not get the raft unhitched from the ship. A short moment later another shipmate, Wayne Neyland, came crawling over. He had a pocketknife, so he cut the straps that held it. Without that knife we would not have been able to release the raft in time, and that raft would have gone down with the ship. At this point I distinctly remember hearing the engine roar as the propellers came out of the water when we crested a wave. In this state of panic and shock I could not help but think, 'Wow, the engine is still running.' As strange as it sounds, I actually felt a moment of pride for the engine that I was in charge of.

As the raft began sliding towards the water, I could see two of my shipmates clinging to its side. Knowing desperately I needed to be onboard, I began my slide over the ship's hull. I'm not sure if it was the keel or the sound gear, but somehow I was projected into the violent ocean out and away from the safety of the raft. The instant I went under water it felt like my chest was caving in and my whole body was being crushed. I didn't know it at the time, but the waves from this typhoon were said to be 60 to 70 feet high, and after sliding over the hull I immediately ended up underneath one of these violent towers of death. Frantically, I clawed and thrashed in a desperate attempt to make it back to the surface so I could breathe again. Even with a life vest on my attempts seemed hopeless. I was completely helpless as I was tumbled under the water like a pair of pants in a dryer, for the strength of this shifting brine was mind-boggling. I was truly a powerless insignificant entity amidt this tumultuous monster of Mother Nature.

After being held under water for approximately a minute and a half, my breathing muscles began involuntary spasms that sucked seawater into my lungs. At this point my instinct to survive kicked into high gear, because my mind only focused on one thing and repeated it over and over, 'I need to catch my next breath.' I honestly thought I would go unconscious and drown before I reached the surface. But, my mind stayed focused on that one thought, 'I need to catch my next breath.' Nothing else existed in my entire world at that moment except that one thought. It was the only thing I had left. For without my next breath, I would cease to exist. I knew as long as I was conscious there was only one thing for me to do with my life at that time. I had to continuously fight for my next breath, because my next breath could be the doorway to the rest of my life, whereas without it, my life would shortly end. Only after the most intensely passionate and strenuous struggle of my life did I finally breach the surface. Before I could inhale I had to cough and projectile seawater from my lungs. After a couple of intense hacks, I was able to draw my first breath. In that instant the open air became the most beautiful and welcomed ally I could have ever asked for. In between my intense hacks I was able to suck in enough air to keep myself conscious. However, at this point I was not too sure I was going to survive because of the amount of water I inhaled. In order for my lungs to be cleared out my coughing grew so intense that it was becoming increasingly difficult to breathe. Even with my head above the surface, this coughing actually had me thinking I would drown anyway. After a short while the hacking cleared enough water out of my lungs so that my breathing came much easier and without interruption. As a result, I was able to concentrate more on my surroundings.

Above the surface, the whipping sea spray stung my face like tiny needles perforating my skin, but I paid no attention to it. I knew I was too close to our sinking ship and fear of its undertow taking me down with it motivated me to swim away. As I looked back at the sinking ship one of my shipmates was still on board attempting to send a distress signal to another ship off in the distance with a hand held portable lantern. Because of this light I was able to catch a glimpse of the life raft's silhouette. Without him attempting to send that signal, I never would have seen it. I immediately began swimming in that direction. As I paddled my arms and legs, I felt like I was stationary. I did not think I was making any progress, but I kept at it anyway. It took me about two minutes to swim less than one hundred feet before I finally reached it. I knew that this five by nine foot canvas wrapped piece of balsa wood with wood slats for a floor was the only protecting barrier between my life and the deadly sea. It was not much of a buffer, but it was all I had. And, as insignificant as it was amid this natural fury, I embraced it as if I were a kidnapped child being returned to his parents. I pulled myself inside. Already inside were the two sailors I saw clinging to the raft when it went off the side of the ship. It wasn't long before another one of my shipmates reached the side and pulled himself in as well. With about four of us in the raft already, together we began paddling the raft in the direction of the voices that were screaming for help. We had no sooner counted off nine of us in the raft when a towering sixty–foot wave came along. When we were about eight to ten feet from the top of the wave, the 120m.p.h. hurricane wind blew the raft off the water and through the air like a piece of cardboard, and nine men flew horizontally into the next trough. Once again I found myself underneath a sixty–foot wave, feeling my chest being crushed and fighting for my life. And, like before, I struggled for nearly a minute and a half, and inhaled more sea water before I breached the surface, hacked some of the water out of my lungs and drew in enough air to keep me conscious. Even with my head above the surface, the coughing made me feel like I would drown anyway. It was nearly impossible to gain a full and satisfying breath of air with water in my lungs and the frightening, violent coughing that had my breathing muscles on the verge of cramping up. I did not know how much more of this abuse was in store for me and I was not sure I would be able to withstand another dunking like that. I was exhausted, out of breath and I thought that if I get pulled under again, I was not too sure I would be as fortunate as I was the first two times. I was beginning to think that I might not make it, but I fought on anyway and never gave up. There was nothing else to do except fight on. When the only thing left between your survival and death is the strength your body has left, then you use that energy until it runs out. Even when my energy seemed to run out, I somehow managed to find more of it. I am not sure exactly where it came from, but somehow it was there when I needed it. I know much of the strength to fight on came from the thought that I might not get to see my son, Richard, grow up. The thought of my wife Ida having to raise our son alone fed me strength that I never knew I had. I wanted more than anything to see my family again.

Through a grueling effort, I again reached the raft. When I arrived a couple other shipmates were already onboard. As I lay inside trying to catch my breath, we could hear the cries for help from our other shipmates who were still fighting against Mother Nature. Paddling to them in this weather was nearly impossible. So, instead, we would get as close to them as we possibly could, then form a human chain. The anchorman would hang onto the raft. The second man would hold his legs and extend his body, as far out as possible, then the third man would hang onto the second man's legs. We were able to grab men who were further out and struggling to make it back to the raft. Each time we picked up another man our chain would grow longer. Each time it grew longer it made it that much easier to reach out and grab those who were further away. After about an hour, we had all nine men back in the raft only to be blown apart by the hurricane winds again. Fortunately for me I was only sent under the waves twice out of all the times we were blown apart, and every time we were blown apart we quickly learned how to form our human chain and make it back into the raft.

After being hurled several times like a deck of cards, we figured out that if we hung our bodies completely out of the raft and reached over the rim and grabbed onto the webbed flooring, it gave the raft a much more dependable firmness. It was only after this move did the lengthy job of dragging sailors one by one back into the raft cease. Now, when we were tossed and tumbled by the wind and the waves, all nine of us were still hanging on to the raft. It was a very rough experience, but the alternative was worse. We maintained this position for several hours and we all knew under these circumstances that this was our best bet for survival. This was as good as it could possibly get at this time. On some of the tumbles we would end up on our backs starring up at the turbulent sky, and on other tumbles we would end up underneath the raft and we would have to crawl out quickly and grab the webbing again before we crested the next wave. My arms were growing so tired that I was no longer able to hang on with just my grip, so I had to wind the webbed flooring around both my wrists. In this case I was not hanging onto the raft as much as the raft was hanging onto me. My right hand was wound so tight that after a couple of hours I did not think I would ever be able to use it again. All the feeling and strength were squeezed right out of it. However, I would not release it because I knew that separating from the raft was a guaranteed death. All I could do was eat the pain and wait for the storm to come to a conclusion.

It wasn't until daybreak that the storm subsided enough for us to climb into the raft without fear of being tossed out. This was a relief, because my arms were mostly useless at this point. Hanging on to the raft for dear life sapped every bit of strength that my arms could possibly hold. By this time they reminded me of well-cooked spaghetti noodles. I could hardly move them, and they could no longer hold me up. It took about an hour to get at least a little bit of my strength back, and the less I used them the quicker my strength returned.

Normally, inside the raft, there were enough sea rations and water to last about fifteen days, but at some point during our troubles all our supplies were lost including our signal pistol and shark repellent. At one point while I was underneath one of those sixty–foot waves I bumped into a keg of water. I thought we might need this later so I wrapped my arm around it and tried to swim to the surface. The weight of the keg held me down, and in a panic I released it. Frantically I made my way back to the surface.

It was in the early hours of the morning when the brunt of the storm began to dwindle. We weren't out of harm's way, but we were safe from the towering waves and high winds that had battered us all night. It was still a dangerous place to be, but it was only about half of what it was at its peak. Ironically, I had a moment to reflect. I thought to myself that if I tried to tell a friend or a loved one about what had taken place in the last few hours, they would never believe it. This was stuff that only bad dreams were made of and stories from someone's imagination. In fact, until I experienced it, I could never have come remotely close to even imagining what the reality of this nightmarish storm would really be like. Nobody could survive what we just went through. How could I explain it when it was truly unbelievable. It was the type of experience that even the greatest imaginations could not conceive of. The reality of the experience far surpassed any impression the imagination could conjure up.

I was also wondering what we would see, or what we might see, as the sun came up. Would we be able to see land? Would we see any passing ships? Would we see any aircraft overhead? All I could do is sit and wait in anticipation while hoping for a paramount rescue. When the sun finally did rise, all my questions were answered. None of these were in view. The only thing I saw were my eight shipmates on a tiny raft in very choppy water, and we were moving up and down with the swell of the ocean and the waves. There was not the slightest hint of any help on the horizon for three hundred-sixty degrees.

In fact, our situation seemed to go from appalling to horrific when the sun came up. We hoped to see some rescue ships patrolling the waters nearby. As it turned out, the only thing patrolling the water were twelve very large sharks that began to circle our raft. They appeared to be anywhere from eight to fourteen feet long. They just hung around us as if they were waiting for something to fall out that they could eat. Wayne Neyland had his pocketknife with him and he pulled it out to try and stab one of the sharks as they passed by the raft. We told him not to because we were afraid that the blood from the shark would wash up on the side of the raft and the other sharks would attack the raft. We did not know anything about shark behavior and we did not want to find out if sharks would attack a raft with blood on it. We knew that if it were not for the raft at that moment there would, more than likely, be a feeding frenzy with all the sharks eating all of us. Learning shark behavior at this time was something we were definitely not interested in.

For hours none of us would move for fear of causing the sharks to strike at the raft or even worse, one of us. We sat motionless as long as we possibly could. The sight of a large dorsal fin passing within four feet of me was without a doubt an extremely intimidating experience. The blank look from their eyes and the length of their bodies were truly menacing. Seeing them from a safe place such as a picture does nothing compared to seeing them in person when you are potentially their next meal. I never knew they were so large or so scary. In school I remember hearing that sharks could grow up to twenty feet, and seeing them in pictures hanging upside down on fishing boats. That really meant nothing to me at that time because pictures do not convey the reality of meeting them in person. When I saw the first large shark swim past the raft with its mouth partially open displaying its razor sharp teeth, a warm rush of fear ran right up the back of my spine and I about hyperventilated. I wanted to panic and run, but with nowhere to run I was forced to grab hold of myself and relax. However, I never really relaxed, I just controlled the explosion of panic that was running through me.

These sharks were not just swimming around the raft. They were also swimming underneath the raft. Since the bottom of the raft had wood slats in it, it was mostly open and one of the dorsal fins rubbed past the bottom of Freeman Hetzer's foot. Freeman very quickly lifted his leg and controlled himself, because I am pretty sure he was feeling the same surge of panic, with nowhere to run, that I was feeling.

As we sat motionless, one shark decided it was going to give the raft a little nudge. It came up from behind us and actually lifted its head partially out of the water and ran into one end of the raft with its nose. This shark was so large that it felt like we had been rear ended by a moving car. It jarred us enough to where we had to grab on tight to keep from falling out. I was so terrified that every time the same shark would pass by it looked as if it had grown another foot to me. The longer they lingered, the larger they appeared to grow. I knew that was not possible, but I was so scared that it sure appeared to be that way. I never really knew these large fish were actually so horrifically frightening.

I could not help but think that we survived the worst of the typhoon only to be eaten by sharks the next morning. It just did not make sense to me. Silently I asked God to lead us through this because we all had family waiting for us back home and I think that the news of us surviving the war and the typhoon only to be eaten by sharks was just a flat out catastrophe. None of us wanted this to be our fate, so all we could do is continue to remain motionless and completely silent at this point.

These sharks were definitely scoping us out as a possible meal. I just prayed that none of us would be their next meal. They would circle the raft, and then come in close as if to take a better look. They would then swim away as if they were leaving. Our hopes would go up as we watched them swim away, and then go right back down when we would see the dorsal fin turn around and come back toward us. Effortlessly they would glide through the water toward the raft. Just when we would think they were going to bump the raft again, they would descend and go underneath or turn and go around. They moved through the water as easily and gracefully as a hawk would move through the air. This was their world and they new exactly what to do in it. We were just nine unlucky souls who were completely out of our element and caught in the shark's element, and we had no idea what to do to get out of it. It was such a paradox to see such a beautiful and graceful creature up close and personal, and know that its grace and beauty were equally matched by a very deadly and aggressive nature when hungry.

Stiff and motionless with fear, none of us moved. We did not want to give any of these creatures a reason to rise up out of the water and pull one of us down under. There were so many sharks around us that even when some of them appeared like they were going to swim away, we would be focused on the ones that continued to linger around the raft. When the ones that were lingering would start to swim away, the ones that were further out would turn around and come back. It reminded me of shift changes on a job site. It was a horrible experience to say the least. I could not believe that the nine of us would have to sit completely motionless for who knows how long. It seemed to be the worst form of torture that could ever be given to any human that had ever walked the face of the earth. I knew that eventually we would become tired and want to sleep. Then what? Would we fall in the water and get eaten? Or, would we be rescued before we became that tired? I did not have the answer to these questions, but I did know that it was, without a doubt, the most stressful circumstance I had ever been placed upon in all my life. Even the typhoon was not as bad as this because I knew we had a chance if the ship went down. With a life vest and the raft on board we had hope. But, being surrounded by giant meat eating fish and not being able to get away, defend myself or move for who knew how long was enough to stop my heart right in its tracks.

Ironically, as several hours passed we realized, and hoped, they were not going to strike the raft and we became more comfortable in their company. It took the whole morning and the early part of the afternoon, but we eventually began to move freely in the raft. At first very cautiously and then more worry free. We finally just accepted their presence as part of the environment and lived with them like they were living with us.

We continued to scope the horizon hoping so see a passing ship or some other type of rescue vehicle. The more we did not see one, the more frustrated I was becoming. 'Why hadn't they started a search for us yet?' I wondered.

We needed to be out of these dangerous waters or we would be shark bait. I was beginning to feel some intense frustration at this point. 'We needed to be picked up and out of these waters at this point,' I thought. Shortly thereafter, we spotted a couple of ships in the distance. They appeared to be patrolling the waters about eight to ten miles away from us. They were moving parallel to us and we could see them when we would crest the rising waves. They seemed to be patrolling for survivors in an area about where they thought we might be. I do not think they anticipated how strong the wind and currents actually were through the typhoon, because if they were looking for us we were actually about eight to ten miles further than where they were looking. The wind blew us out of the raft so many times during the night that we seemed to pick up a few more miles in travel than the military calculated. Besides the wind blowing us, the speed of the current with those giant waves also added to the great distance we traveled during the night. How I wished we had a flair gun at that time. Just one flair was all we needed and I knew we would be rescued, but we did not and I decided to quit torturing myself with all the things we did not have, because all it did was add to my already insurmountable frustration.

We kept hoping that one of these ships would turn and start heading directly at us, but it never happened. All we could do is watch them patrol in the wrong area. The level of frustration I was feeling was beyond words and something I had never experienced before. I would pray to God and ask for one of these ships to turn and see us. When it did not happen I would get angry with the Navy and question their intelligence. Didn't they know we were right here and not where they were patrolling? What is wrong with these guys? Turn the ship and head out this way. I felt like I was driving myself mad, so I quit thinking about it.

Since we did not see any rescue vehicles passing directly by us, we decided, as a group, to start looking around for useful objects that might be floating nearby. We spotted three yellow onions. The nine of us leaned over the side and began paddling with our hands as we looked out for the sharks. The sea was still very choppy, rough and uncertain, so it took us nearly two hours to get all three onions on board. We decided that if we ever grew hungry enough we could eat these onions to help curb our hunger. We also picked up a wood section of slat board that we thought we could use as an oar when necessary. That was about all we could do to help ourselves at that point. Everything else was up to the navy, Mother Nature and fate. However, I never forgot mother's lessons on faith to all of us kids when we were growing up. At this point I continued to have what I thought was true faith on this first day. I continued to pray and ask God to let us be rescued. Then, I would become frustrated when we were not rescued. As the sun was closing in on setting, I almost could not believe that the navy had not picked us up yet. What the heck were they doing? Didn't they know we were floating out there waiting to be picked up? They had to know something when our ship did not report in earlier that day. As far as I was concerned, they should have had every ship in the area looking for survivors, and we had not seen a single ship pass directly by us, except for the ones that were off in the far distance patrolling the wrong area. I was very upset at this concept. How dare they not send more search and rescue efforts. I figured since they knew the direction of the typhoon, they would be able to figure out the general vicinity of where they could pick up survivors, or about where they would be in comparison to where their ships went down. However, that was not the case on day one. We just continued to float, drift, wait and hope that we would be picked up soon. I was noticing that my frustration was beginning to turn into anger, and anger was something that I did not need to experience at this point in my real life nightmare. It just seemed that the more I thought about our circumstances and questioned why we were still floating in the ocean, the more my frustration turned to anger. Anger was something I was not used to, but it seemed to be slowly taking over. The only thing I could do to keep it under wraps was to continue to look for a rescue vehicle on the horizon and hope that we would be picked up soon. If I did not hang onto hope, my anger would take over and the next thing I would know is that I would be very, very angry. I had to force myself to keep hoping. Otherwise I would have nothing left but debilitating, useless, draining anger.

It wasn't until the end of the first day that the storm finally began to calm down. The wind subsided and the turbulent ocean settled. As night approached, I realized we were coming up on our first twenty–four hours of drifting on this beautiful ocean that now seemed so harsh and dangerous. I could not help but think that we were just a speck on this huge expanse – invisible to any eyes of search and rescue. I began to feel insignificant on what seemed to be an endless blue carpet in every direction, because we had no idea of where we were or where we were headed. The only thing that I knew for sure is that we were somewhere adrift on the Pacific Ocean and finding a needle in a haystack would definitely be easier than finding us. Maps of the Pacific Ocean that I saw in school were just a reminder of what we were floating in the middle of, and the recollection of that was not very encouraging. The Pacific Ocean was always the biggest looking object on that map. It is quite a strange feeling to be caught under these circumstances where your life is literally on the line. You know that death is tapping you on the shoulder, but you do not want to turn around and see what it wants. My mind kept going back and forth between what seemed to be a cloak of lingering death and a spec of light that symbolized survival. Up to this point I had never been in a position where it was just my thoughts and my self. There was nothing else I could do except sit and listen to the chatter that took place in my head. I had never noticed it before. I just kept going between hope, panic, fear, frustration and hope again. It seemed to me that the hardest thing I had to deal with was not knowing what was going to happen. The fear of the unknown was taking me between a total peace and an extremely intense panic. Not knowing was something I had never faced before and I did not like it at all. At this point, all I could do was to force myself to focus on my prayers and continue to hope. It was definitely an internal battle that only I knew about, and nobody else could do anything about it.

The evening of the storm I was kept awake all night for obvious reasons. I never knew that being tossed around and beaten by wind and water could be so ruthless. I was used to breathing air and feeling the breeze gently massage my skin on a cool summer night, not having it contort my body as it hurled me through the sky like a leaf. Water I was used to floating on, swimming in and drinking when thirsty. I really did not comprehend its ability to nearly beat me senseless with its turbulence. On night two, I had another sleepless night, not because of the storm's uninterrupted abuse, the storm had already passed, but because of the aberrant situation we found ourselves in. I never would have thought that, after avoiding any German U-boat attacks in the Atlantic and entering the Pacific at the time of Japan's surrender, we would have much of anything to worry about or even have to deal with. At times I was having trouble believing that the current situation we found ourselves in was even real. A couple of days ago we were sweeping the waters around Okinawa Island cleaning up the mess that was left behind by the war efforts. There was no more war and there were no more enemies. Yet, here we were fighting a new enemy. The very thing that sustains our physical life was on the verge of sapping the life right out of us, the earth. Many thoughts of home began to cross my mind. I thought of my wife Ida, and wondered if I would ever see her again. I thought of my newborn son Richard, and wondered if he would grow up fatherless. I thought about my mother, my father and all of my brothers and sisters. More than anything, I wanted to see them at this moment. If I were the richest man in the world, I would have given up every penny I had just to be with my family again. It was this day that I learned to never take anything for granted, especially my family members. I wanted more than anything just to be with them and see their faces. I wanted to hug my wife and hold my son. I wanted to thank my parents for everything they had done for me. I wanted to tell my brothers and sisters how much I loved them, but I couldn't, because I was stuck somewhere in the Pacific Ocean on a tiny raft with eight of my shipmates, and they were the only family I had at the time, and there was nothing any of us could do.

Day Two

CHAPTER 2

The water finally settled down on the second night. However, there was nothing we could do. There were no reference points on the horizon to paddle toward, so all we could do is just sit in the raft and drift aimlessly without a clue of where we were headed. Maybe on the second night we would be able to see a glow on the horizon indicating land and civilization, but instead it was all black. We really hoped that we would run into something, like a landmass, or a ship, or a buoy, or anything. But, we ran into nothing and the only thing we saw was the black ocean meeting the starry sky in all directions.

When the sun finally set on the first day of being in the raft, we entered our second night. Although we were in an ominous and very dangerous situation, the conditions on the second night were much more welcomed than that of the first night where it took every bit of strength we had just to hang onto the raft in order to stay alive. We hoped to see a beacon of light from a passing ship, so we were all very unsettled and alert hoping for a sighting, but it never happened. The nine of us were alone with nothing to do but sit, hope and wait. I looked around at my shipmates who were all very still and quiet. There was Cullinan, whose real name was Thaddeus Martin Cullinan Jr. He was an F2c, fireman 2nd class. Also on the raft was Hartman, whose real name was Donald Raymond Hartman. He was an S1c, seaman 1st class. Next to him was Hetzer, whose real name was Freeman Theodore Hetzer. He was a GM3c, gunners mate 3rd class. Next to Hetzer was Hicks. Everybody called him Bob, but his real name was Robert Charles Hicks. He was a coxswain. Next to him was seaman 1st class Mendello, the Italian boy from New York. His full name was Joseph Francis Mendello. Next to him was Neyland. He was the one who cut the raft away from the boat with his pocketknife. His full name was Wayne Bernard Neyland, F2c, fireman 2nd class. Next to Neyland was Plumb. His full name was Norman Wolcott Plumb. He was a motor machinist 3rd class. And lastly, other than myself, there was Renner, whose full name was Elmer John Renner. He was the only officer of four that made it to the raft.

The nine of us were just sitting, waiting and not saying a word. To me it seemed that this was a place in my life where time and patience clashed like two mighty warriors in battle and I was caught somewhere in the middle. At times I wanted to become insanely angry, but a bigger part of me knew that that would not make a bit of difference. We had no power to change the situation and no control over our circumstances. We could not do anything about it. Waiting to be rescued and not even knowing if a rescue was going to happen is an extremely trying experience that was beginning to spark a battle within myself that I never knew could happen. I was beginning to feel an intense panic that I had never experienced before. It seemed to come from somewhere in my unsatisfied anxiety. I had to fight this feeling. I had to ignore it, but sometimes it was difficult. A big part of the frustration came from my thoughts that kept telling me, 'I cannot believe the navy has not come to rescue us yet, don't they know we are out here waiting for them to pick us up? What is taking them so long?' Adding to my high level of anxiety was the constant threat of big sharks patrolling around the raft. At night it was much more frightening because we could not see their dorsal fins or where they were in the water. At least in the daylight if a shark decided to rear its ugly head and try to pull one of us in we could see it coming and at least have a chance to defend ourselves. However, at night we would not be given that advantage. If a shark decided to reach for one of us, we would not know it until it was too late and its teeth had sunk deep within our flesh. This thought kept the hair standing on the back of my neck. I had to force myself not to think about what it might feel like to have my flesh perforated by those scary teeth.

As the night wore on, we would hear something splash in the water right next to us and one of us would say, "I think there is one over there." We could never see them, but we could hear them, or at least we thought those sounds were sharks. It could have just been the water, or not. We never knew for sure. Night made the shark experience about a thousand times more intense. It was what I imagine being blind must feel like. You cannot see them but you know they are there, because you can hear them. I would rather have been bull whipped than be under those circumstances. It brought the meaning of stress to a whole new level that felt like it was out of this world. I never really knew what stress was until this evening. When there were long periods of no noise coming from the water around us I would somewhat relax. Then, all it would take is one tiny splash for me to tense right back up again and remember we were surrounded by several, giant meat eating fish. It was tormenting, but after several hours in the dark, the noise seemed to finally disappear. I was hopeful but cautious. I knew they were still in the vicinity. They probably just went a little deeper and passed under the raft. However, it was a nice break to think they had actually stopped patrolling the surface. Maybe they grew hungry while they were waiting for one of us to fall in the water so they could eat us and, instead, went in search of fish food somewhere deeper, or better yet, somewhere else. At least that is what I hoped actually happened.

We had now gone twenty–four hours without water, and we were all unbelievably thirsty without a single drop of fresh water to drink. We hoped that maybe it would rain that night, but of course it did not. There were no clouds above our heads, only stars. In contradiction to the dangerous situation we found ourselves in, it was quite peaceful in our serene drift and if we were not in fear of dying it would have been pleasant. The scenery is what I imagine an overnight fishing trip would be like with my buddies had it not been for the unsheltered cramped quarters on the raft, the dire need for thirst quenching liquids and our ill state of affairs.

Without any light nearby, the sky was brilliant with millions of sparkling stars. I never knew that the ocean held such beautiful scenery within its grasp, unlike the detestable scene it held us in. On board our minesweeper, while out at sea, I had noticed the stars previously, but on this night I was seeing them in a way I had never noticed before. The enormity of God's creation, I wondered. How could something so perfect and beautiful be so lethal? The more I thought about nature's deadly beauty the more I would panic from my dreadful anxiety. So silently I began to pray. I thanked God often for my Christian heritage. I prayed for help, and that we would be rescued soon. I looked back and thought about some of my past times of prayer. No sooner had I uttered the last word of each prayer, my mind would go into high gear of why the navy was letting us drift in the open sea with thoughts of 'no one cares.' The panic that would start to settle in my mind was sometimes scary and overbearing. Part of me wanted to panic to the point of the purest, most fantastic insanity I could ever imagine. Even though we were in the wide-open ocean with no barriers to limit our drift, at times I felt like somebody with claustrophobia who had been stuffed into a tiny closet with no hope of getting out. I think I experienced the purest form of hopelessness that could ever be felt. It was only after I was on the very edge of losing control of my mind, the verge of insanity, that I embraced, perhaps, the most valuable lesson of my life. That night I learned how to take charge of my mind and use this very important God given tool to keep my sanity. I realized I had no control over my circumstances at this point, but I did have total control over my mind and my internal choices. I could choose to embrace worry and anxiety or I could choose to release it. With all that had gone on in the last twenty-four hours I had been taken to a psychological place I never knew existed. I was actually battling my own thoughts. I was not dead. I was relatively safe, but the majority of the thoughts that entered my head seemed to be hopeless, negative and depressing, all because of this awful situation we were caught in. With this new discovery I decided I had to redirect my thought process in order to keep the negativity out of my head. So, I took my mind off of our current situation when I began to develop good long thoughts of my past. When I would start to recall a certain event from my life, I would take it all the way to the end in every detail. My thoughts would take shape like a tree with branches. I would start at the trunk of the tree, then branch off in certain areas. By doing this I was actually able to recall past events I had previously forgotten. When I would make it to the end of one memory I would go back to the trunk of the tree and start the branch of a new memory. Fortunately there were enough memories to occupy my mind whenever I needed it. I noticed this newly discovered survival tool was most effective at night, because during the day it was much more difficult to focus with the sun beating down on my head and body all day. Eventually, it was in the sun and the heat that some very vivid hallucinations began to pollute my mind, but at night, the lower temperatures made it much easier to concentrate.

The first memory of my childhood I remember recalling was truly the earliest memory I could actually bring to mind. I was about two and a half years old and I was sleeping in the hallway of our home with my brothers Luke and Red. We had to have it this way because we were a poor family with nine children in a two-bedroom house that might have been 800 square feet. My mother and father had one room and my older sisters shared the other room. The rest of us had to sleep on the floor. This particular night I was sleeping in the hallway just outside my parent's room. Suddenly, I was awakened when somebody stepped on my stomach. I let out quite a loud groan when this happened. It turned out to be a burglar who had crawled in through one of the windows. As he was sneaking through the house he did not see us sleeping in the hallway. Unknowingly he stepped on me while he was unable to see in the dark. The groan I let out was so loud that my father woke up in somewhat of a panic. As he made his way out of his room the burglar began to run. My father was able to grab a large Caribbean conch seashell we had in the house and smash the burglar in the back of the head just as he was jumping back out the window he came in. My father hit him so hard that he ended up breaking about three inches off of one end of the shell. My father then ran around to the front door and chased after the burglar, but the burglar was too fast. My father was unable to catch him as he very quickly ran away.

Father came back into the house to make sure everything and everybody were okay. He checked me to make sure I was not hurt, but I was just fine. When I let out that groan the burglar lifted the pressure off of my belly. I do not think he had any intention of hurting anybody. He just wanted to find something of value that he could steal and sell in order to make some pocket change. However, he left our house without any valuables and I am sure he had one heck of a whelp on the back of his head, because a conch seashell is not an easy thing to break. This man had to be running on pure adrenaline after being hit on the back of the head as hard as he was.

Since we did not have a telephone my father was unable to contact the authorities. It took about twenty or thirty minutes, but everybody in our household finally settled down and we were able to get back to sleep. After the way my father reacted to that burglar we all knew we were in good hands. We knew our father was a good protector. With that in mind we all went to sleep and had a very good night's rest.

The next day, father did visit the authorities and give a description of the individual and what happened. There was not much they could do at that time, but they thanked my father for the information and said they could use it if something like this keeps happening in the area. After all, most burglars tend to stay localized and hit as many places as possible in their designated area.

As the memory of that particular thought came to an end, I picked my head up and looked around. It was dark without a moon and the stars were as brilliant as always. My eight other shipmates were just sitting there quietly in their own little worlds. Not wanting to use up any energy unnecessarily by talking, I leaned my head back, closed my eyes and began another thought that took me back to my childhood. I was still very young and this memory was not too long after the burglar incident. I remembered playing outside of the house when my father came up to me and said, "Bill, your overalls are pretty dirty. I'm going to take them to the oilfield and have them steam washed." Since I played outside in the dirt all the time my once blue overalls were literally black with encrusted caked on dirt. Being such a young child I had no problem with it. Dirt never bothered me. It was the only childhood playground I ever really had to myself, and it was my favorite toy. The next day, my father took my overalls to work with him and steam washed them. Since my father worked in the oilfields there was a steam washer there. This washer was used for successfully removing layers of stubborn oil off of the workers' clothes after a day or two in the oilfields with oil raining down on them. If it could remove stuff that obstinate, my father knew it would have no problem removing a few weeks of embedded soil.

When he brought them back I almost did not recognize them. They actually looked blue again which was something I had completely forgotten about. At first I thought they were a new pair until my father told me they were the pair he had taken to work and cleaned for me. It was something very simple, but I was actually very excited and happy to be wearing such a good-looking, clean pair of overalls. Of course it did not take me long to encrust them with dirt again. But, when they did become filthy my father would take them back to the oilfield where he worked and steam wash them again.

When I was done with this particular thought, it branched off into another thought that I had not remembered for a while. I remembered one day my father did not come home from work at his usual time. He actually showed up quite a bit later. When he finally did come home his right hand was wrapped with some very large bandaging. He had been at the hospital having his hand worked on, because while he was at work with a crew drilling another oil well he had an accident. While he had his hand on a piece of oil pipe that was standing up inside the tower, the traveling block, which is used as a counter weight to lift the pipe up through the tower, came down on his hand and instantly severed his right thumb. He was rushed to the hospital and the doctors did what they could, but my father was never to have a right thumb again. This was pretty tough at first being that my father was right handed. But, he did adjust and he was just grateful that it was not worse than it actually was. He said at least he did not lose a limb or his life. He was a strong man with a very positive attitude.

Both my parents were very positive. We lived in the poor part of town and right next door to us was the segregated part of town where all the Afro-Americans in our area lived. Even though there was a great deal of prejudice in our area and across the country at that time, my parents were very good about teaching all nine of us to treat all people equally. My parents were just as respectful to the Afro-American folks as they were to anybody else. In return my parents were very respected by a group of people who were disliked, shunned and looked down on by the majority of the population at that time. They referred to my father Jack as "Uncle Jack." And they referred to my mother Zella as "Aunt Zella." Over the years that we lived there, my mother was a mid-wife to over thirty births in that segregated part of town. The Afro-American folks were extremely grateful for her selflessly giving of her time to help those who were too poor to afford a doctor or a hospital. At the same time, my mother was grateful that God used her for such an honorable service to a group of people who deserved much more than they were handed. My parents did not see color. They saw character. What a person did meant more to my parents than what a person said. They never judged a person by their looks, but they did judge them by their actions. Both my parents were treated with great respect and they also gave a great amount of respect.

I remembered every time we would walk into that segregated part of town we would pass Aunt Ellen's house. She was a 95-year old Afro-American woman and she was always sitting on her front porch in a rocking chair. She always had her cup of whiskey in her hand no matter what time of day we would walk by. One day while I was walking with my mother she said to Aunt Ellen, "Aunt Ellen, one day that alcohol is going to be the death of you." Aunt Ellen responded with, "Oh no Mrs. Zella. It won't get to me because I weakens it." Being so young at the time I did not understand what she meant, but mother explained to me that half of what she was drinking was whiskey and the other half was water. Aunt Ellen was 95-years old and still doing pretty good. She could still get around on her own and she still had a very sound mind. At 95, Aunt Ellen was in better shape than many people were when they were 60. In the middle of this particular memory I could not help but think, 'I hope I make it to the age of twenty-five,' because being where we were at this time was not looking very promising.

Sitting in the back of my head at the end of every thought was the reality of those predators that were somewhere around the raft. Although I had not heard one splash for quite a while, I was still very aware of their presence. I knew that if one of us fell in the water there would probably be a better chance that the unlucky one would not make it back into the raft. All I could do to forget about this reality for a short while was begin another thought from my memory tree.

My next memory took me back to the age of about six years old. Since we were so poor growing up in the middle of the great depression the only toys I had was the dirt I played in, my imagination and two glass medicine bottles. The medicine bottles were used to hold cold and flu medicine. When the medicine was all used up my mother gave them to me so I could use them as cars. They were about six inches long, an inch and a half thick, two or three inches wide and they had about a two-inch neck on them. They made wonderful cars in my imagination. I would sit in the field near our house and play until it was dark. Even in the dark I would not stop playing. Where we lived there were fireflies everywhere. I called them "Lightening Bugs." When it became dark I would catch a couple of those bugs, smash them, smear their light chemicals on the front and back of my bottles and use their light making substance as head lights for my cars. They were bright enough to actually illuminate the ground in front of my imagined cars. I would play until my mother would call me to come home. When you do not have much in terms of material objects, it is amazing what your imagination can do. At the end of my playtime I would take my two bottles and place them in a specific spot on the back porch. That way I knew where they were and I could always find them. I sure enjoyed those two bottles.

I remembered one time while I was outside playing in the dirt field I used tree bark, twigs, dirt and rocks to build an entire town. This town had a fire station, a hospital, a church, a school, a park and homes. I used my glass bottle cars to make the roads that connected all the different parts of town. While I was building it my nephew Benny showed up. He was my oldest sister's son and he was always a thorn in my side when we were kids. He had a way of getting me in trouble and getting me "whoopings" that I actually did not deserve. On this particular day he showed up and watched me while I was building my town. He did not help, he just watched. He must have sat there and watched me for thirty minutes while I finished this town that took me at least two hours to complete. Suddenly, with both his hands, he methodically destroyed every part of my town in just a matter of five seconds, and then he turned around and started running away from me. I was so angry I chased after him. I knew that when I caught him I was going to make him pay. As we were running I was gaining on him slowly when he turned up a trail that headed toward my house. At this point I knew I was not going to catch him in time so I stopped and picked up a very large dirt clod and hurled it at him. As he was running I caught him right between the shoulder blades and it sounded like a big 55-gallon drum being hit. He fell over on his face crying. When he stood up he could not catch his breath because the impact knocked the wind out of him. Hitting him with that dirt clod instantly released all my frustration and I was very satisfied with the outcome. As far as I was concerned we were even. Although I knew that when he made his way into my house and told my mother what happened I was going to get it. With that in mind I decided to stay outside as long as I possibly could. Eventually it was too late for me to be outside any longer and I had to go face the consequences of my actions. My mother gave me quite a whooping that evening for my actions, but I have to say after remembering what he did and seeing him receive his just reward with that dirt clod, it was the most enjoyable whooping I ever received from mom. It was a painful one, but it was well worth it!

As I drifted out of my memory state of mind I looked around. I could see the faintest hint of light beginning to rise on the horizon. It was still too dark to see anything around us, but I knew it would be getting brighter in the next couple hours or so. The stars were still out, and the sky was a clear brilliance. It was absolutely beautiful and I could not enjoy even a second of it. I felt the frustration begin to rise in me again. Not wanting it to get the best of me, I closed my eyes and went back into my memory tree. My next memory took me back to the second grade. I was sitting at my desk when my teacher Mrs. Theada came up to me and said, "Bill, I want you to go with my husband. He's going to get you something." Wow! Great! I thought he was going to get me a toy or something like that. Instead he took me to the shoe store and bought me a pair of shoes. When I would go to school Mrs. Theada would see that I never wore shoes. That is because I did not own a pair of shoes. That particular day, when Mrs. Theada approached me, it had been snowing and there was about three inches of snow on the ground. This was the first pair of new shoes I ever owned. I was once given a pair of girls shoes by our neighbors the Cains that looked like they could be boys shoes, but I was so used to going around barefoot that they never felt comfortable on me, so I never wore them. After Mr. Theada bought me the shoes I would wear them to school. I was so unfamiliar with shoes on my feet that I literally had to learn how to walk with them. It was very strange to me. In fact it was so strange that I would take them off when I would walk home, tie the laces together and sling them over my shoulder. When I would leave in the morning and walk the mile and a half to school, I would keep the laces tied together and hang the shoes over my shoulder. Just before I would arrive, I would put the shoes on. I did not want to insult Mrs. Theada. After all, it was a very kind act to buy me shoes when she thought I needed them. What Mrs. Theada did not understand is that I was so used to not wearing shoes that walking in the snow did not bother me at all. My feet were so callused that they never became cold enough to catch my attention. However, I did keep those shoes until I outgrew them.

Thinking of those shoes brought me back to the memory of the night our ship sank. I had to kick my shoes off because they were creating too much drag and weight while I was trying to swim in the water. I was able to maneuver a little easier in the water without the shoes on my feet. I was not the only one who was barefoot. My eight other shipmates were barefoot as well. They probably had the same experience I had while fighting the current.

Not wanting to spend much time thinking about our current situation, I went back into the memory tree. My next thought took me back to grade two. While I was in the second grade I remembered that marbles were the things to have. If you had marbles you were sought after. The more marbles you had the more popular you became. As a second grader, I had quite a few marbles in a small container. One day while I was sitting with my brother Luke, who was two years older than myself, Buck Pashaw came by, reached into my container and took a handful of my marbles. Buck was the school bully. My brother Luke immediately said, "Buck! You put his marbles right back where you got them." Luke and Buck were the same age. Buck answered back with, "I ain't never going to give his marbles back to him." Now my brother Luke was one of the nicest guys you could ever meet, but I never knew him to back down from a fight, and I never saw him lose a fight, and this particular day was no exception. Luke stared Buck down, then hauled off and punched him square in the face. Buck went flying back and landed on his backside and my marbles went flying everywhere. I remember the marbles went flying so high that they seemed to fall out of the sky for fifteen minutes. I had to run all over the place just to pick them all up again. It seemed to take all day to get all my marbles gathered up again. Buck, who thought he was a tough guy, found out that he was not so tough. He went off in another direction crying his eyes out. I never knew anybody to stand up to Buck like that and if they did, I never expected it to be my own brother.

After the dust settled and the marbles were all picked up, Luke and I continued on with our marble game. Ironically, within a couple of days, Buck became my best friend and we happily played marble games together without so much as a hint of a conflict. He also became pretty good friends with my brother Luke. It sure is strange how that works.

My thoughts were interrupted with the arrival of dawn. I knew it would be getting sunny soon so I just kept my eyes closed as long as I possibly could. Part of me kept hoping that when I opened my eyes I would awake from this nightmare that had already gone on far too long, but the non-delusional part of me knew that would not be the case. I knew that when I opened my eyes I would have to face a situation that I would not wish upon anybody in the whole world for any reason. This was not the place for any human anywhere at any time.

When the sun finally began to rise, it was the second day of our ordeal, and there was not a cloud in the sky for as far as the eye could see. As we looked around in hopes of seeing some help from a passing ship, or anything for that matter, we sighted something that did give us some hope. We could see the peak of a large hill, or a small mountain, on an island off in the distance some twenty-five to thirty miles away. Excited, we all began to paddle. Some of us paddled with the wood strips we picked up the day before, some of us used our hands, and some of us took the wood slats out of the netting that made up the flooring of the raft. We were energetic and enthusiastic in our effort. We knew we were going to make it and be safe now, so we rowed and paddled our hearts away. In fact, we rowed ourselves to the point of physical exhaustion, but we did not let that hinder us. We continued on and paddled through the exhaustion by ignoring it. However, after several hours of this continuous effort, the mountain on this island seemed to grow smaller and smaller. It seemed that we were actually working against the tide, and the only way we were going to defeat it is if we had a motorized raft. Unfortunately, we were not afforded that luxury. There was nothing any of us could do except sit, wait and hope. Once again the powers of nature made us insignificant entities among their treacherous surreal beauty. I almost could not believe this was actually happening. Safety was in our sight, but far from our grasp – so close and yet so far. Some of my shipmates grew frustrated and angry at the idea of having land in sight but unable to reach the safety of it. Some of them were cussing and cursing at the situation. The more I listened, the more I realized it was not the situation they were cursing at as much as it was the lack of control we all had over this ominous circumstance. Strangely, I myself had no anger at that time. I was no longer allowing myself to grow frustrated. Too much frustration could turn to anger, and anger would not help the situation. In fact, it would hurt the situation by expending valuable energy that could be used as a possible survival source later. With that in mind, I had no other choice but to let things be as they were. I just made the choice not to think about it. I noticed that it was the thinking about it that seemed to start any panic, anxiety or any other problem for that matter. The less I thought about our current state of affairs the less worry and anxiety I felt. It was at this point in our journey that I realized the importance of not thinking. If there were no thoughts to trigger my emotions, then I had no imaginary problems. At that exact moment I could still breath and my body was still alive. Other than being thirsty I had no problems at that very moment. Since water was not an option I ignored my thirst as well. With so many things out of my mind I honestly had no problems at that time. With this in mind I just sat and waited. At night I used the memories of my past to get me through the evening. During the day I was learning to use my lack of memory and lack of thought to help me through the sun scorching days.

Being just a couple weeks past August, it was blistering hot with no clouds and the sun beating down on us. After just two or three hours in the sun I was beginning to notice how sunburned my skin was becoming with no shade in sight. All I could do was sit there and let it burn. My skin was growing sore as I slowly took on the look of a tomato. As I looked around at my shipmates I could tell they too were tormented with the same anguish that I was suffering. I was definitely not alone in my misery.

We were not talking much, because there was not much to talk about. We spent most of the time quietly as we drifted up and down with the swells of the ocean. At the top of the swells we could see off into the horizon. At the bottom of the swells all we could see were the swells that surrounded us. All day long we went up and down. At times it was almost relaxing, but I found it extremely difficult to find any real comfort in the calm of this gentle ride. We remained quiet and calm as we rode the gentle swells. Occasionally, one of us would say something, another would answer, and then we would all go quiet again. We continued that way until later that day, in the middle of the afternoon, when we heard a plane approaching. It was very high going directly over our raft – a B-24 Liberator, an Air Corp bomber, and it must have been at least 5,000 feet above the surface. We yelled, screamed, waved our arms and splashed the water, all in hopes that they would see us, but the crew never saw us. Our thrashing and yelling dissipated as the plane continued on its course slowly fading out of sight and earshot. After it was completely out of sight, one of my buddies made the remark, "Let the air force go, they never help the navy anyway." It felt like we were just taken on a very high momentary high and dropped right on our faces with a thud. They were so close and if only one crewmember had seen us our entire circumstance would be completely different. We would be out of this dangerous mess and I would be on my way home to see my family, I thought. When I noticed myself playing, and thinking the "If only" game I immediately put a stop to it. This was a sure way to frustrate myself to the point of insanity. Instead, I stopped thinking and put my trust in the Lord. I said a prayer, then waited. I figured if it was my time to go home to heaven, then so be it, but I still had a much stronger urge to want to go home and be with my family. I was not ready, or willing to leave them yet. Once again, all I could do is sit, not think, wait and hope for the best.

We all went back into our silent states for the rest of that day. We were all sad, worried, disappointed, but hopeful. No matter what happened we knew we could not give up hope. It was the only thing we could hang onto in this out of control environment where the only thing that was certain was uncertainty. We were at the mercy of Mother Nature and I really began to understand the lesson of not being in control of my own destiny. I knew that no matter what decision I made, I was not getting off that raft and going home anytime soon.

I also noticed that the sharks were still lingering. They were not surrounding the raft like they had before, but they were still in the near vicinity tagging along as we drifted. At this point I definitely knew they were just waiting for one of us to go over board so they could grab an easy meal. However, I made it a point that I was not going to be that easy meal they were waiting for.

As the sun set it was a welcome feature at the end of the day. My skin was burned a shade of red that I had never seen before. A couple of times I pressed my finger against the skin on my arm. It would push the blood out of the piece of skin that my finger was pressed against. When I would quickly remove it I could see the contrast between the natural color of my skin and the sunburn, then the blood would rush back in and turn my white skin a dark red. By the end of the day it was quite a contrast. It was extremely sore. When I touched it, it actually hurt. I was becoming very uncomfortable physically. I never knew the sun could be so debilitating with it beating down on me all day. I had taken the shade for granted and never realized how helpful and protecting it actually was. How I wished I had an umbrella for a reprieve from the now repulsive pounding sunlight. At times the heat was so unbearable that I had to cool my skin off with the ocean water. Its cooling effect did not last long, but it was all I had and better than doing nothing at all.

As the sun dipped out of sight on the horizon that evening, I realized we were beginning our third night on the raft without water, food and little to no rest. I was so thirsty that I wanted to pray for rain more than a rescue, but the more I thought about my thirst the more thirsty I seemed to feel, so I just continued to ignore it. There was no use in torturing myself with something I had no control over.

Nighttime was a break from the relentless sunlight, but it was no exception. Instead of dealing with the unbearable heat, we had to deal with some uncomfortably cold temperatures. During the day our sea soaked clothes were somewhat of a radiator at times, but during the evening those radiators sucked heat out of us that we really did not want to lose. At the height of the evening we were usually shivering. Some of the guys would sit on the netting at the bottom of the raft and partially submerge themselves because they said it actually felt warmer in the water.

The third night on the raft I had not slept a wink. It was quite difficult to sleep under these dire circumstances. That evening I had positioned myself on the edge of the raft. While sitting there, with the lack of sleep that I had, I unintentionally fell asleep and flopped back into the water. It is amazing how quick water can bring a person right back to consciousness, especially when they know the water they are in is infested with giant sharks. I think I walked on water that evening. I immediately woke up in such a panic and mad scramble to make it back into the raft that I grabbed the side with my weak arm, and with one yank I pulled myself head over heels right back into our little refuge. Those were some very large sharks and they never stopped patrolling around our raft, so I knew they were close by. I had never been so scared in all my life. Even being caught inside the typhoon was not nearly as scary as that brief splash in those dangerous waters. The thought of a shark sinking his finely honed teeth into my fleshy body was despicable to me. I felt very fortunate that I did not have to encounter any razor sharp teeth from one of those ferocious looking man-eaters that evening. After that experience I decided to sit inside the raft with my back supported by the inside wall. It was less than ten inches from the surface of the water, but it was better than falling back in. I was finally able to grab a little bit of sleep that night, without a big concern of becoming shark bait.

Day Three

CHAPTER 3

I drifted in and out of sleep for several hours that night and never really caught any solid rest. With my eyes closed, it seemed more like somebody was turning my head off and on. The sound of the ocean water slapping the side of the raft would be interrupted with what seemed to be brief moments of nothingness. Intermittently, I would go between the resonance of our surroundings and what seemed to be an oblivion that had happened to me many times before while going to sleep. Usually, this oblivion would win out, I would dream and get a full night's rest, but this simple pleasure was now an impossible task to fulfill considering the bedding I had been provided. All night long I was rocked asleep, then rocked awake.

I did not visit my memory tree this night due to the stage of fatigue I was experiencing. My body was much too exhausted to expend any effort on thought processing. All I could really do is grab catnaps all through the night and hope that all these shallow sleeping spells would all link together and create a moderately decent night's rest. At times I could not stay awake, but at the same time I could not stay asleep. It was quite an annoying contrast. This went on until the eastern horizon began a gentle glow. The luminous shine of the waking sun was letting me know that we survived our third night on the raft while lost somewhere in the Pacific Ocean. I was still alive, but at the time there seemed very little to be happy about.

As the sun rose at the start of the third day parts of our bodies were soaked in salt water for nearly seventy-two hours now. I personally was constantly soaked from the waist down up to this point. I did not think much of it except at night when the water allowed the cool air to extract my body heat, thus causing me to shiver. But, at the dawn of day three, I started to notice sore spots on my lower half. Through the first half of the day the sore spots began to mutate into round, red, painful bumps. There were so many of them concentrated in some areas that it looked like I had been shot with shotgun pellets. Eventually, some of them filled with pus and began to take on the look of large pimples. Before the day was over, some of the white head sores ruptured with an abundance of painful stinging and burning as well as a fair amount of oozing pus mixed with a little blood. I had no idea what they were and I had no idea what to do about them. All I could do was try not to touch them or aggravate them in any way.

In addition to these sores, due to my short sleeve t-shirt, the exposed sections of my skin were beginning to go beyond sunburn and take on the appearance of a dark purple and black look. My skin started off with the usual sunburn red to a darker red, then it turned dark purple and eventually black. As I looked around I noticed my shipmates were going through the same skin color changes. It was painful to touch so I just avoided contact with my own skin if I could help it. I was slowly learning that exposure to seawater and sun for extended periods of time was a very slow, but extremely torturous experience on the human body. I had no idea that these two items of nature, which are usually pleasant, could be so damaging and harmful. They seemed to be slowly digesting me. At this point I was beginning to understand the importance of shade and dry skin. I would have given almost anything to have an umbrella and dry clothes at that time.

As I looked around I was also noticing that a white salty substance was beginning to ooze from our eyes like streaking tears. If we wiped it away it would just come back, so we just left it alone and let it be. We figured it was not going to harm us any more than we already were so we just ignored it. But, it did look like we were all crying white tears. My mouth was dry and parched. I could not even muster up saliva to moisten it. My lips were a little swollen and beginning to crack. I did not have a mirror, but if I wanted to get an idea of what I looked like all I had to do was take a look at my shipmates, because we were all having the same symptoms.

On this third day, our strength was leaving us at a rapid pace. Even though we tried the best we could, our paddling effort toward the island in view was, at this time, very poor. It had gone from an arduous chore to an impossible task. There was no use in trying because we never seemed to make any progress, but we tried off and on anyway. Some of us figured that if we are going to die out here we might as well die trying. These off and on efforts were demanding and using up what little unspent energy we had left. When we realized this we decided, as a group, to divide the three yellow onions we had picked up three days earlier. We thought that maybe the nutrition would give us the little added strength we would need to continue paddling. However, my appetite for food left me on this day. I had no desire to eat anything. I also knew that the onion would be hot in my mouth and that would only intensify my already unbearable thirst. I gave my portion to the guy next to me, my good friend Norman Plumb. I watched all the guys take the onions. They bit into them and began chewing. I could not help but think that if I was unable to muster up saliva to moisten my mouth, how the heck were they able to. There had to be moisture inside the onion that was doing it for them. When I thought of the moisture inside the onion it was somewhat appealing to me, but the thought of burning my parched mouth with the onion was more discouraging. I did not want to take the chance of intensifying my thirst.

It was very hot going into the afternoon of the third day. It was excruciating, but somehow the toughness of the human body was able to persevere up to this point. I had no idea I could withstand so much physical abuse from Mother Nature. I was surprised to see how much punishment I was able to endure. I just was not sure how much more my body would be able to handle. Our discomfort was rising at an exponential rate, but our bodies were not giving up. I would sometimes entertain the thoughts of which one would give first under these impossible surroundings, my mind, or my body. At this point they both felt like they were in a race and running neck and neck. I could only hope there would never be a finish line in this particular contest.

To preserve our strength, we all stopped talking to each other. We only spoke when absolutely necessary. At this point I noticed some of the guys appeared to withdraw into themselves. They sat on the floor of the raft with their legs crossed Indian style, their arms folded and their head tilted forward. One of my shipmates, Renner, became so withdrawn that we couldn't pull him back even with a good shake and a loud yell. He just sat there in what seemed to be a deep trance that began to worry the rest of us. Occasionally he would come out and mumble something very unclear, letting us know that for the most part he was still with us. It was as if he brought on a self-induced coma that he would come out of once in a while. We were all concerned for him, but we knew there was little to nothing we could do about it. He had to do whatever he had to do to protect his self, and if this was what was going to work for him, he had our full support. We wanted him to survive as much as we wanted ourselves to survive.

As the afternoon passed by in a manner that seemed lethargic, things began to get rough. One of my shipmates was really beginning to worry me with his nonsensical speaking. At first I thought he was kidding, but the more he spoke the more I realized he was serious. Joe Mendello, a kid from New York, kept grabbing my right thigh and calf and squeezing it. Then he would say, "Where did you get that Pepsi? Please, can I have one? I know that's a Pepsi in there." I had to keep telling him that it was not a Pepsi and that it really was just my calf muscle. He did not believe me and he kept asking for the Pepsi that he thought was inside my leg. I had to assure him that everything was okay, but he never stopped believing that I had a Pepsi inside my leg. Even after I pulled up my pant leg and showed him my calf he still thought there was a Pepsi underneath my flesh. I was dreadfully worried for him.

As this day drudged on, desperation was beginning to set in. Mendello was beginning to scoop up the seawater and drink it. It doesn't take long for salt water to kill a person once they are dehydrated. I did not know exactly how long it would take, but I thought it would only be a matter of hours before bad things would begin to happen. Obviously his parched mouth, and maybe the onion were getting the better of him. I think I used the word "No" over a hundred times that afternoon in hopes of deterring him from essentially poisoning himself with seawater. It got to the point where I had to wrap both my arms and legs around him in order to hold his arms at his side just to keep him from drinking it. The instant I would relax my grip, real quickly he would scoop up some more and drink it before I could stop him. He knew that drinking salt water was dangerous, but his level of thirst was so intense that any common sense and logic seemed to be overridden by a very powerful and desperate primal instinct to survive. There was nothing I could say and very little I could do to prevent him from drinking the caustic, deadly brine.

As I was holding him back and listening to his mumbling nonsense, I could not help but think that this must be what happens when the frustration, panic and anger win out. I kept feeling like I was battling insanity by not thinking, and I never really crossed the line into insanity, but Mendello seemed to give up and quit fighting the frustration and anger. It was quite frightening to see this happening before my eyes. I wanted him to be okay so he could make it home. But, it seemed our circumstances and mainly the seawater was beginning to win out. I held onto him as much as possible, because there was nothing else that could be done at that time.

When evening came there was no serious delirium among the nine of us. Some of us were beginning to hallucinate, but we had not completely lost it yet. Those who did not drink the seawater were much further from losing it, while those who did drink the seawater tended to say things that did not make a whole lot of sense. I was getting a little worried for the ones who were beginning to lose it. Joe Mendello was having the toughest time. My good friend Norman Plumb was also beginning to make no sense. Ted Cullanan was also lapping up seawater early on and he was beginning to mumble nonsense. I was becoming very scared for my shipmates. I did not like what I was seeing and I did not like this experience. I did not know what was going to happen at that time, and it was a very depressing thing to have to watch.

The sun setting on the third day marked the beginning of our fourth night in the raft. This was definitely the most difficult night so far. Even though I did not drink the seawater, I felt myself bordering on delirium and

I had to work much harder at keeping the nighttime positive mind thought pattern headed in the right direction. It was all I had and the only thing I could do to preserve what little sanity I had left.

As I went back into my memory tree I remembered a time when I was eight years old and I was playing with my good friend and neighbor whose nickname was "Snow Ball." He was an Afro-American kid who was the same age as myself, and he lived in the black part of town that my family lived right next door to. One day while we were playing outside my house, mother called me into the house for something I had done to one of my younger siblings that I should not have done. When I made it into the house, my mother grabbed a switch and began to tan my backside. There were many times I received a whooping from my mother for doing things I should not have done, and I was actually beginning to get used to them, so this particular time I remembered I started to cry out real loud and pretend it was really hurting me. When in fact, I was only putting on an act so the whooping would stop sooner rather than later. When my mother stopped, I pretended I was crying. When she though I learned my lesson she let me go back outside. When I made it back outside I noticed my buddy "Snow Ball" was standing there facing me with these large tears rolling down his cheeks, and his eyes were opened real wide. When I asked him what was wrong he said, "Bill, one day your ma ma's going to kill you from all these beatings you get." I assured him it was okay and that I was just putting on an act pretending that it hurt as bad as it sounded. His tears dried up and we continued playing like we were before my mother called me into the house.

"Snow Ball," had a very interesting haircut. His whole head was shaved except for one little tuft of hair just above the center of his fore head. My other neighbor friend, Sammy Cooper, had an older sister who was married to a man named Alexander. Every time Sammy's sister showed up to visit her family Alexander would come with her. Every time Alexander saw Snow Ball he would pull out his pocketknife and chase Snow Ball around the yard telling him he was going to cut his tuft of hair off his head. Snow Ball was terrified of Alexander and would tell me how much he did not like him. When Alexander would catch Snow Ball he would just hold him and pretend he did not know how to cut his hair off. Of course Alexander was just teasing Snow Ball, but that did not matter to Snow Ball. He really did not like Alexander for terrorizing him every time he saw him.

The other neighbor friend I would play with on a regular basis was my good buddy Sammy Cooper. Sammy and I always had a good time playing cowboys. In our imaginations he and I were the toughest cowboys in the history of the world. We would ride horses, lasso bad guys, quick draw and shoot guns like no other. We were truly unstoppable. If we were not playing cowboys, Sammy and I would play football. We would kick, pass, punt and run with the ball like we were the best players in the world. Sammy also had real toys to play with unlike my imaginary toys. Sammy's family had enough money to buy their family three meals a day, clothing, toys and any other necessity. Sammy's father, Mr. Cooper, owned a gas station in town and he always had a steady income despite the Great Depression at the time. Not many people had money, but anyone who owned a car needed gasoline and Sammy's dad had what they needed.

The Coopers were very kind and giving people. When I was about thirteen years old, Mrs. Cooper noticed that I was gaunt and skinny due to the fact that my family was so poor. Due to economics, a square meal was hard to come by in my house, and going to bed hungry was not an unusual event for my family members while we were growing up. The day that Mrs. Cooper noticed my emaciated look she went to my mother and said that she wanted me to go to her house every morning before going to school and drink a warm glass of milk fresh from their milk cow. That is exactly what I did every day, and in a matter of a week or two I started putting on some weight, gaining my strength back and my healthy complexion returned. If it were not for Mrs. Cooper and the Cooper's kindness, there is no telling what would have become of me. I do know that had I continued on the path I was on, it would not have been a positive outcome in the long run. My malnutrition probably would have caused all kinds of problems and diseases in my body.

When I was finished with my current chain of thoughts, I opened my eyes and looked around. My shipmates were mostly immobile and sleeping. Once again the evening was beautiful, but from my perspective it was a deceitful beauty. Between the sunburn and the salt-water ulcers, the physical pain I was experiencing at the time was enormous and mounting. I knew the sharks were still in the vicinity, but my physical pain seem to take precedence at this time. I was actually in too much pain to worry about the sharks. So I did the only thing I could do, I closed my eyes and went back to my memory tree.

I began to think about some more of the good times as a young boy growing up in Orange, Texas. I thought about my wonderful family and the love and togetherness that we all shared. My thoughts went back to the great depression of the late twenties. One Christmas eve, my older sister Floy called all the kids together for a meeting. When we arrived, she began to say, "You know this Christmas will be down for all of us, but we still have each other and that's the most important thing of all. So, lets be thankful for that and try to make the most of our situation. We can still hand make little gifts for each other and for mom and dad."

When my sister Floy was finished with her speech, my older brother "Red" (Royce), who was very creative, went to the back porch and began doing something. We were not sure what he was doing. When he returned a little while later, he had a potato that looked like a dog. He used little sticks for the legs and neck, then walked over and gave it to my other brother Luke, who was two years older than myself, and we all had a good laugh. That Christmas we didn't have anything in terms of monetary value, but we did have the warm feeling of love, togetherness and family unity. I also knew that was something we could never buy and that could never be taken from us. And, under my current situation, as every day grew tougher, I wanted more than anything to be with family again. But, as each day passed, it was becoming increasingly difficult to fend off the hopelessness that was trying to grow within myself. However, I had no other choice. I could not give up at this point, so I continued on with my uplifting memory tree.

There were nine children in our family, four boys and five girls. I had three brothers and five sisters, and an outstanding, strong, loving Christian mom and dad. During the early part of my life my dad was a sharecropper. He never owned a car, a truck or a driver's license. He did what he could do, but during the great depression his options were extremely limited. Most of the time there was nothing he could do to earn enough income to buy everything we wanted. He was able to get us enough food for survival, most of the time, but even that was a tough commodity to come by back then.

In fact, there were times when all we had in the house was a sack of flour. After watching my mother, I knew how to make a lot out of practically nothing at all. That tends to happen when there are no other choices and the basic necessity of food is a scarce commodity. Mother, however, made sure we were all fed with what little she had every day. There would be hot biscuits on the table with brown flour gravy almost every night, and that always hit the spot. Every night I could have easily eaten two or three portions of what I normally ate, but I had to be selfless and think of my other family members. We all made sure that everyone received their fair portion of the meal. Like I said earlier, going to bed hungry was not an unusual event in my house, not just for myself, but also for the whole family.

When the depression hit, my father was no longer able to earn an income through sharecropping. So he found a new job in town working for a local millionaire. My dad would walk three miles, one way, to work every day. He was a handyman, and he did whatever needed to be done around his boss's house. In return, he was paid thirteen dollars a week in cash. My father didn't make much money, but he did earn enough to make sure we were at least fed with enough food to barely get us buy, and that was definitely better than nothing at all.

My attention was taken from my memory tree when I heard a splash. I opened my eyes and somebody had fallen asleep on the side of the raft and fell back into the water. In a mad scramble this person pulled himself back into the raft knowing the predators were near by. I took a few seconds, but after he was in the raft I realized it was Freeman Hetzer. As exhausted and dehydrated as he was, the thought of those sharks taking a bite out of one of us seemed to motivate anyone of us far beyond any exhaustion or dehydration. I personally would have rather died of thirst while baking in the sun than being eaten by one of those demonic looking creatures.

When I saw that Freeman was okay, I continued on with my memory tree. I remembered back to when Roosevelt was elected President. He created the WPA (Works Progress Administration) and the CCC (Civilian Conservation Corp.). To my dad, this meant jobs with paychecks! My dad immediately filled out an application and was hired on the spot. After a week or two of working, he received his first official paycheck in over two years. I could never forget that huge, broad smile on my dad's face when he walked through the front door for the first time in two years with a large bag of groceries in each arm. Oh the joy it brought him just to be able to buy a variety of different foods for his family, and the joy it brought his family. We were finally able to eat three square meals a day without going to bed hungry. It was quite the blessing President Roosevelt granted us. He was a true hero in our family. He put food back on our table.

The W.P.A workers built chemical toilets for every house in the city limits of Orange. Prior to that, we all had a hole in the back yard covered with an outhouse. In rain or shine, night or day, we had to go outside to use the toilet, and when you have to go then you have to go. I used to really dislike having to get up at two in the morning and go outside in the dark without a flashlight just to do a number two inside a very stinky outhouse.

The W.P.A also drained all the swamps in the area finally getting rid of the mosquito problem. They also began paving all the dirt roads in Orange and putting in cement sidewalks along the roads. Before the sidewalks and paved roads were put in, people had to walk down the dirt roads to get anywhere. I remembered my whole family would have to walk three miles to church every Sunday in about three inches of silt. We would be wearing our Sunday best and there would be a big cloud of dust billowing up behind us as we made our way to church. Someone could always tell where our family was. All they had to do was find the front of that giant cloud of dust and there we were. By the time we would make it there, we didn't exactly look like the church going type. Our Sunday best was always covered with a rather thick layer of fine silt. If it were a hot morning we would sweat and have a little bit of mud mixed in with our Sunday's finest dress. We were all just happy that God judged our hearts and not our looks.

When I was about the age of fourteen my dad decided he wanted to move the family out of the city limits and into the country. While we were in the city there was not a whole lot of property around the house and my dad wanted to start his own garden. Since he had a job now and was able to pay a little more in rent, we moved to a house in the country a few miles outside the city limits. There was much more property for my dad to farm his own large garden. The only draw back was that my neighbor friends were no longer close by and we had to trade our chemical toilets for outhouses with holes in the ground. Other than that it was a great decision. However, I sure missed my good friends Snow Ball and Sammy Cooper. When we would travel near the area I would get to see them, but it was too far to walk everyday, so I was forced to play with my family members and use my imagination. Without Sammy there, the only time I could play football is when my nephews would come over and that was not often enough. Living across the street from Sammy I was able to play almost everyday. I sure missed Sammy out in the country.

I opened my eyes again and looked around. It was still dark and my shipmates seemed to be sleeping. When I felt the intensity of my physical discomfort and the shivering I had from the chill of the night, I became clearly conscious of my unforgiving reality again. I went back into my memory tree in order to help me ignore it. I thought about my first job in Orange, Texas at the Texaco station right off of the old I-10 freeway on Greenleif Avenue. I had been working there a couple months when a navy blue, 1937 Chevy sedan drove up and I started pumping gas into it. While I was pumping the gas, the driver of the vehicle said, "Did you hear that the Japs bombed Pearl Harbor?" I had not heard of it yet, so I stuck my head inside the car window to listen to the radio announcement. I almost could not believe what I was hearing and at the same moment, like every other American at that time, I was furious. I remained furious for the rest of that day and into the night. When I went to school the next day I was still furious, as were all my friends. Anger just boiled inside me and I was ready to go overseas and kick some Japanese butt along with every other high school senior at the time.

After December 7, 1941, I knew I wanted to do my part to help our country win the war. But being so young and never being away from home I wasn't sure what to do. So I asked my mother's advice. My mother said that she would pray about it and give me an answer the next day. Mother prayed about everything and always seemed to come up with the most fitting answer to almost any question. The next morning my mother had an answer for me. She said that she noticed whenever somebody enlisted on the east coast they would be stationed on the west coast, and whenever somebody enlisted on the west coast they would be stationed on the east coast. She then said that if I did not want to be too far from home then I should be stationed on the east coast, which meant that I would need to enlist on the west coast.

After my mother's advice I decided to continue to work at the Texaco Gas station to save money for a trip to California in order to enlist in the Navy. As I worked at the gas station the number of military convoys increased dramatically after the start of the war. Sometimes there would be as many as one hundred military vehicles come through at a time that I would have to fill up. They were always on their way to Louisiana to train for the war. This was quite inspiring to me at that time. All these soldiers were preparing to fight the enemy and I wanted to be a part of that in some way or another.

I worked until April of 1942 when I had saved enough money to possibly make it out to California. My final destination was Whittier where my sister Floy was now living with her husband Buddy. With only thirty-eight dollars in my pocket, my mother told me that she had prayed to the Lord and that the Lord told her that I was going to make it out there just fine. She told me not to worry about a thing. Mother always seemed to have a direct connection with God so I trusted what she said.

It was in the last week of April 1942 that I began hitchhiking to California. With my mother and father's prayers, consent, and best wishes, I was on my way. A man in a car picked me up. He drove me down the road about ten miles before he headed in another direction. I was back on the road hitchhiking again. My second ride was in a semi truck loaded with oil pipes. We had driven for several hours when I realized that hitchhiking was not going to cut it. As we were entering San Antonio, Texas I told the driver to let me off as close to the Southern Pacific train station as he could and I would walk the rest of the way. The driver answered by saying, "It is two A.M. and I will drive you to the station." This turned out to be an answer to prayer, because the station was much further than I expected. It was at least ten miles from the point on the highway where I asked him to drop me off. I was sure glad he was a kind person.

He drove me right up to the front of the station and let me out. I thanked him and he said he would not leave until he knew that I had purchased a ticket and that I would surely be on my way. I walked into the station and purchased a ticket to Los Angeles, California for thirty-four dollars plus tax and other fees. I had two dollars and forty cents left. I went outside and showed the truck driver that I was signed sealed and delivered. He was comforted. I thanked him again, and we parted ways.

With only two dollars and forty cents in my pocket, and four days before I reached Los Angeles, I wasn't sure how I was going to eat. When the train stopped at another station in the later morning, another prayer was answered when a young army soldier boarded the train and asked if the seat next to me was taken. I said no, and he sat down next to me. I noticed he had a big bag with these green things in it. I asked him what they were and he told me they were avocados. I had never heard of them before, nor had I seen them. It was one of the strangest looking fruits I had ever seen in all my life. He also had a loaf of bread with him. So we made a deal. I would buy the drinks and the coffee with my two dollars and forty cents and he would share his avocados and bread with me. That is exactly what we did and it worked out perfect for both of us. By the time we reached Los Angeles I had thirty-five cents left and I developed a real liking for avocados. In fact, I could not wait to find some for myself and eat them between two slices of bread.

Upon my arrival in Los Angeles, I purchased a bus ticket with a transfer to Whittier. The ticket cost me twenty-five cents. The bus drove and stopped at many stops. I knew I wanted to get off in Whittier. I was not familiar with the area, so when I heard the driver yell the word Whittier, I pulled the cable to get off the bus. As the bus drove away, I realized I was standing on the corner of Whittier Boulevard and Atlantic Avenue. I was in East Los Angeles about ten miles short from the city of Whittier. I knew my last dime would not be enough for another bus fair, so I decided to go into the corner drug store I was standing next to. Since I played trombone when I was in school, I thought I might be able to pawn off one of my three Orange High School band metals for twenty-five cents, but the man inside said he had no use for them. Not sure exactly what to do, I went back outside and stood in front of the drug store. In a short while a very friendly man walked up and introduced himself. We began to talk and I explained my dilemma to him. He said, "I'll bet if you step on the next bus and explain to the driver what happened, he'll probably let you back on." So, I waited for the next bus. When it arrived I stepped on board and sure enough, when the bus driver heard what happened, the man was right. The bus driver let me on without any trouble whatsoever.

When I arrived in Whittier, I used my last dime to call my sister. I remembered back to what my mother told me, that I would have just enough to get me out there and I would be just fine. By golly, my mother was right again. As far as I was concerned, it was a miracle and my mother knew it was coming. I had the exact amount of money to take me from Orange, Texas to Los Angeles, California without a penny to spare. I loved the fact that mother was right again, and the Lord was watching out for me.

With that thought in mind, I came out of my memory tree and into my stark reality. I could not help but think at that time, If the Lord was watching out for me back then in a much less dangerous situation, then I am sure he is watching out for me under this much more deadly situation. And there has to be a reason as to why we have not been rescued yet. If the Lord were going to take care of me with the easier stuff, then he would definitely take care of me with the more severe stuff. Even though this thought crossed my mind, it was still very difficult to maintain my faith with all the discomfort, pain, thirst and fear I was experiencing at the time. So, I closed my eyes and picked up where I left off.

My sister gave me instructions on how to get to her house. She said that Buddy would also come and meet me. I was just a few blocks from their house when Buddy picked me up. It was great to see him and we exchanged hugs. I always loved Buddy because he was such a truly kind man. It was always exciting to see him and I was very happy to be in his presence again.

Upon my arrival, after exchanging hellos and hugs, because it had been quite a while since I had seen my sister and Buddy, the first thing my sister Floy told me was that there was a young lady at church she wanted me to meet. I said that would be just fine. After an excellent dinner and very good conversation, I went to bed and had an excellent nights rest. All that traveling made me pretty darn tired. I honestly think that I fell asleep before my head hit the pillow and the next thing I remembered was waking up the next day feeling completely invigorated and rested.

The very next morning Floy took me to church and introduced me to an absolutely lovely young lady by the name of Ida Mae Campbell. As soon as I saw her I was immediately attracted to her. She also seemed to be equally attracted to me. We talked and talked and just could not stop talking to each other. I thought she was the most beautiful woman I had ever seen in my life, and I was magnetically attracted to everything about her. As time went on, a very short time, Ida Mae turned out to be the love of my life. It was hopeless for both of us, and we knew from day one that we were right for each other. I knew it was definitely in God's plans that Ida Mae and I were meant to be together. We courted for just a couple of weeks when I proposed to her. She said yes! We were both elated and we knew it was the right thing to do in God's eyes and in our eyes. I never knew a simple guy like me could ever be so incredibly happy. Finding love in California was one of the last things on my mind, but when it happened I was absolutely just fine with it. It was wonderful. I never knew that finding my true love would be such a beautiful experience. There were no words to describe how jubilant I really felt. This experience gave a whole new meaning to life for me. My love for Ida Mae opened up passageways to a delightful set of emotions I never knew existed. My life took on a whole new direction and a whole new purpose at this point. Our affection and love for each other seemed to take off like a rocket. In fact, I was bragging so much about her to everybody that my parents decided they had to meet this young lady that had me spellbound. My mom and dad came out to California and gave their wholehearted approval of this wonderful

Christian girl. And, even if they had not approved, I was a lost cause, but I knew they would. Four months later, on August 14, 1942, we were married. When I met her, she was Ida Mae Campbell. After our wedding we were both Mr. And Mrs. Herbert Ralph William Harrison.

Ida and I rented a small one-bedroom house at the rear of another house on Milton Avenue. The Army draft board was on my tail and I heard that the Union Pacific Railroad was one of the first lines of U.S. Defense in the country. My brother-in-law thought that maybe I could get a job with the railroad, do my part for my country and stay at home with the love of my life.

The railroad hired me and I was able to do my part for my country and go home to Ida at the end of every workday. But, it was not long before the progression of the war brought a change to my perfect situation I found in California. My mother wrote me to say that they had received my draft papers back home in Orange, Texas and the Army was going to draft me. I was concerned that there would a good chance I would end up in the infantry. I really was not interested in the infantry after meeting and marrying Ida Mae.

Day 4

CHAPTER 4

As I partially opened my eyes, I could see that morning was waking at the opening of the fourth day and the nightmare continued. Even though we could see the tip of a hill on some island in the distance, we were still lost in the Pacific Ocean. With the exception of the guys who were sipping on the seawater, the ones who did not drink the seawater had not had a single drop of water to drink for four days now. As a result, the intensity of my thirst was enormous, and I had to fight the urge to drink the salt water. I clearly knew that would guarantee certain death, and I was in no way giving up. I had too many people that loved me and too many people I loved that I wanted more than anything to see again. I had to struggle against the thoughts of being completely surrounded by water that I could not drink. After witnessing some of the behaviors from some of my shipmates after they drank the water, I had no desire to have the same thing happen to me. I wanted to keep my wits about myself as long as possible. Even if I died, I wanted to die with my wits intact as much as possible.

These circumstances were more like being surrounded by an ocean of beautiful poison. All I could do to ignore it was revert back to my memory tree. It was the only help I had, so I closed my eyes and picked up where I left off.

Upon word of my draft papers arriving, I made the choice to join the navy. Two of my brothers were already serving in the navy. My brother Luke was in the pacific onboard a sub-tender supplying a group of submarines, and my brother Royce, nicknamed "Red," was also in the pacific onboard an ammunition ship named the "Pyro." My younger brother Claude eventually joined the Navy when he reached legal age, but he was still in basic training when the war ended. That meant all four of the Harrison boys were in the U.S. Navy at the same time while W.W. II was still in action.

The day after I received word from my mother, I went down to the nearest recruiter's office and filled out all the necessary papers. Of course, they did not take me immediately, so I had a chance to visit the family in Orange before I was sent to basic training. I figured if I am going to go off to war in the near future, I might as well give one last visit to all my family members back in Texas.

I went into the Union Pacific office in Los Angeles and asked them if we could work out some type of deal. I did not have enough money to pay for two round trip tickets for Ida and my self, so I thought that since I did work for them that maybe I could work one of the tickets off when I returned back to California. When they found out I wanted to visit my family in Texas before I was sent to basic training for the Navy, they said they would arrange two free round trip tickets out of respect for me going into the military to fight the war. In my eyes, this was another miracle in my life. That truly was a very kind gesture. That sure did help me out financially as well as morally.

Ida and I had a wonderful time seeing all the relatives. It took a little time for Ida to get used to the outhouse out back. We had no indoor plumbing so she was not very fond of the two holes we used out back for our toilet breaks, especially when she found out she had to pass through the chicken yard. The chicken yard was full of many surprises that she did not want to step in. Life in Orange, Texas turned out to be a bit of a challenge for my beautiful city girl. Being from the city, she had no idea that people could actually live that way. Watching her out of her element was quite entertaining to say the least.

In addition to the challenges at home, the three-mile walk to church sometimes seemed like it was up hill both ways for all of us. For Ida, it was flat out an unpleasant experience with her city girl high heel shoes on. She learned real quickly how hard it was to walk three miles with the wrong type of shoes on. We all had to walk to church because my dad never owned a car or a driver's license. The family was used to it, but I do not think Ida was ready for this somewhat rugged country life being right out of the city Whittier, California.

Upon seeing the old church again, it reminded me of some of the fun times we had in my childhood years. My brother Luke was a sleepwalker. One Sunday night, while Luke was lying down on the bench he fell asleep. Halfway through the pastor's sermon, he stood up and started to walk to a bench at the front of the church. Mom told dad to go get him. Dad turned to mom and said, "You go get him." What made the whole thing so funny was that Luke stood up and faced the audience with a great big grin on his face while he was sound asleep. He stood there for a few minutes with this grin while the whole audience's low chuckle gradually turned into loud laughter. They could tell he was sound asleep with his eyes open. My parents were very amused. He finally made his way back to the bench and sat near my parents while he was still sound asleep. When he finally woke up, he could not remember any of it.

With nine siblings in the family, dull moments were not a part of our life. It would get real noisy at the close of the service when everyone was asked to stand. Most of us kids would lie down on the benches and fall asleep. As much as we loved going to church, there were times when it was just flat out boring for us kids. There were always one or two who would not be given enough room to lie down, so we felt it was our duty to tie the shoestrings together of the ones who were sleeping. At the end of the service when the congregation was standing up to leave, it was quite a funny sight to see when the sleepers would stand up and try to walk. One would fall and cause a chain reaction like dominos, and they would all end up on the floor half asleep, and unsure of what just happened. Of course what goes around comes around and I had my share of falling asleep, waking up and falling on the floor. It was all done in fun and in the end we would all have a good laugh.

At the conclusion of this memory I did not bother opening my eyes. I knew the sun was coming up and I was afraid that if I opened my eyes I would just see what had already been there for the last three days, an honest to life nightmare. Instead, I just kept my eyes shut and continued on with my childhood church memories. Reliving them was much more enjoyable than my current reality.

One Sunday morning at church, my brother "Red" (Royce) decided he was going to leave church early. That morning, after the service ended, the rest of us were given a ride home on the back of a flat bed truck. While we were driving home, my brother Luke saw Red up in a persimmon tree about twenty yards off the side of the road. With his slingshot, Luke shot at Red from the back of the truck while we were doing about twenty-five miles per hour. When we arrived home my mother asked if anybody had seen Red. My brother Luke said he saw Red up in the persimmon tree we had passed and that he shot a rock at him with his slingshot. About that same time, we noticed a big cloud of dust coming across the field behind our house. At the front of this dust cloud was Red. He was running, he was angry, and he had a very large welt right between his eyes. When Luke realized that he actually struck Red between the eyes, he took off running for his life. Luke ran through the house. About the time he was going out the front door Red was running in the back door. Red never caught Luke that day, and that was probably a good thing. However, after enough time passed Red cooled down and Luke was able to approach him without fear of physical punishment. All I remember thinking is that Red was two years older than Luke, but it was a good thing Luke was a faster runner than Red, or I think Luke would have paid for his lucky shot with some very large bruises.

During my high school days, after we moved out to the country, we lived next to the railroad tracks. It didn't take long for word to get around on the railroad route that the family in the big old two story, unpainted house would feed all hobos who asked for a meal. Even when there was not much to eat mom always managed to find a meal for all who stopped by and asked. The hobos who stopped by were truly grateful for my mother's generosity. These guys were usually down on their luck and they were having a rough time in their lives, but that did not matter to Mother, she enjoyed giving the needy what they needed. She did unto others as she would want them to do to her had the roles been switched. My mother was truly an excellent example of how people should treat other people regardless of social class.

At this point in my hellish experience I could only hope that the good deeds of my mother would be reciprocated and I would make it home to see her again. I hoped. I kept telling myself that it had to be worth something. Mother's good karma had to rub off on me. If it rubbed off on me, then the rest of us would benefit.

Besides the thirst, sunburn, saltwater sores and sharks, there was one more problem I was beginning to notice. My appetite that had previously vanished was returning with vengeance. My stomach cramps redirected my attention from my memory tree for a short while. I wanted to say something about my stomach pain, but earlier we made a pact that we would not talk about food, water, or anything else that we thought would make our situation more difficult. Therefore, I had to refocus my mind, and not wanting to leave my memory tree I continued with my past.

After a whole month of fun and good times, Ida and I were on the train heading back to California. Upon our arrival, it was a mad scramble to move Ida and all our belongings in with her mother. We managed to achieve this task within a couple of days and I was able to relax knowing that Ida would be safe and watched after while she was with her mother. That was very important and comforting to me. I needed to know she was safe before I headed to basic training. We were also pleasantly surprised to find out that Ida was pregnant with our first child, which was another reason for me being concerned that Ida be watched over while I was going through basic training.

I was sworn into the Navy October 28, 1942. With this memory, I could not help but think, 'Would I have been better off if I joined the Army?' Probably not, because I believed that God was in control and everything happens for a reason.

My swearing in took place on the front lawn of the Los Angeles City Hall. The Navy and the city of Los Angeles randomly picked our company of recruits on this day for a special occasion. They had the Rudy Vallee Band playing patriotic music. The master of ceremonies was actor Leo Carillo. There were about one hundred-fifty recruits who were sworn in that day, and all of us together raised our right hand and gave an oath to our country. When we were finished giving our oath, I felt honored and proud. We were given a brief moment to say good-bye to our loved ones and shortly thereafter, we were all put on buses and shipped to basic training in San Diego, California. Because of the progression of the war basic training was nothing like it is today. We spent a total of twenty-one days there, which is one-fourth of what it might be today. By chance, it just so happened that the recruits in the hut next to ours had actor Henry Fonda in their group. Henry Fonda was a big movie star back then, and me being from the little town of Orange, Texas had never seen a real life movie star. I really wanted to see if he looked the same in person as he did in the movies. I would sit outside my hut sometimes and get to watch Mr. Fonda wash his clothes and hang them up to dry. We did exchange a hello a couple of times, but it was never more than that. There were two things I found out after these experiences. One, that he looked the same in real life as he did in the movies, and two, he was just another person like any other recruit in basic training that wanted to do his part in the war effort. The movies tended to canonize people, but now I knew better. He was just another man.

I also had the opportunity to meet pro-golfer Sam Sneed and I even managed to play a round of eighteen holes with him. He played the entire course with a five-iron. Needless to say, he beat me on that course pretty bad. I considered myself a pretty good beginning golfer before that experience. After playing a round with Sam I realized I had a long way to go and a heck of lot more to learn. I was nowhere near as good as I thought I was.

Richard Hanna was in our group and slept in the bunk right above me. Later in life, Hanna became a congressman in Washington D.C. who represented Orange County, California.

I actually did hang around quite a few renowned people while I was in basic training. I did not really notice that until I had the chance to think about it on the raft. However, it was not until many years later that I knew Richard Hanna was to become fairly well known for politics in our area.

Our stay in San Diego seemed to go rather quick, and three weeks later, our basic training was completed. I was sent to the Destroyer base in San Diego, California. Several of my buddies from basic training were assigned to ships heading to the South Pacific. One week later, my name was called out over the P.A. system along with fourteen others. There were fifteen of us in a draft heading for Miami, Florida. Mother was right again! I was moving closer to my family in Orange, Texas by receiving orders to work in Florida.

There was a twenty-four hour delay in Los Angeles the day I was supposed to head out to Florida. As a result, I received permission to go see Ida. She was only twenty miles from Union Station, so I headed to her mother's house. Not exactly understanding what the orders meant or what my final destination was left a question mark with both Ida and myself. We both decided once we figure out what is going on, then maybe she could come out there and stay with me or at least come and visit as much as possible.

I arrived in late November with the group of fourteen other guys. Upon our arrival, we were assigned to the Navy Base Fire Department, Pier I. I was going to be a naval fireman, and that was just fine with me. Being newly married and with an expecting wife I would much rather be a military fireman in the States than a military soldier fighting over seas or somewhere in the ocean.

I was in Miami for a little more than six months when I received word that Ida gave birth to a healthy baby boy on June 17, 1943. We named him Richard. I was ecstatic, and I could not wait to meet him. I remember the first time I saw him I absolutely fell in love with him. He was the most beautiful human being I had ever met, and he was perfect. It was at this moment that I understood the true meaning of pure unconditional love. Once I met my son, I knew I would not hesitate one second to give my life if it meant protecting him so that he could continue on living a full life. It truly was an unbelievable emotion, and words could never describe the euphoria I was experiencing. I had no idea that having a child was the most incredible, indescribable, most perfect feeling I had ever gone through in my whole life. At this point I could not help but think that God made the birth and life of our own children the sole purpose for our existence. It was amazing to say the least.

Shortly after Ida recovered from childbirth, I was fortunate enough to have both of them move out to Miami with me. Every day I would come home from work I could not wait to sit with Ida and play with Richard. I was a naval fireman in Florida that came home to his wife and child everyday after work. What more could I ask for. My situation was a perfect symbiotic relationship, and I could have done this for the rest of my life, or at least until the end of the war. But that would not be the case. We were together for a whole wonderful year when I received orders to replace a sailor out at sea. Suddenly that one-year seemed far too short. I could not get enough of my new family, and there was nothing else I really wanted to do except be in their presence. It literally broke my heart when I had to send Ida and Rich back to California while the Navy shipped me out to Boston, Massachusetts. I had a new meaning in life. I had a family that needed me there. I was no longer interested in going over seas to perform my part in the war. I wanted to do it as a fireman in Florida, but that did not matter. The military had other plans for me, and there was nothing I could do to change that.

Almost begrudgingly, I was sent to Diesel school to learn how to operate diesel engines. The only thing I could do was put all my spare time into hitting the books and studying just to minimize the pain I felt from having to send my wife and son back to California. Keeping busy was the only thing I could do for myself. As a result, I became pretty good at studying and I finished ninth in my class. I was really very happy with that. Refocusing the energy from my broken heart into the books actually gave me a little something to feel proud of. I did better in the military school than I ever did in the public school. I actually walked away from that school feeling like I could do the things that I previously though I could not do.

When I completed my courses at Diesel school, my next assignment was Little Creek ANF – Navy Base Little Creek, Va. I was only there for two weeks when I was given orders to head to Jacksonville, Florida to put into commission the YMS-472. I was going to be a plank owner, and I met a great bunch of guys on this ship who were also going to be plank owners. There were thirty-two enlisted men and four officers that would be running this 135-foot mine sweeper through the dangerous waters of the Atlantic Ocean. We knew the German wolf packs were out there, but we all knew that we would be just fine. I was excited about my new journey, but I profusely missed my wife and son.

I was actually going to be on a brand new ship. The YMS – 472 was built by the Gibbs Gas Engine Company of Jacksonville, Florida and was commissioned at the yard on November 10, 1944. After two weeks of ship fitting and taking on supplies, we were put out to sea and heading up the east coast. Our skipper, an excellent navigator and leader, put us through many drills, calls and rehearsals to battle stations. This was a good thing, because on our first night out at sea, around 2:00 a.m., we were awakened by the battle stations alarm. As we manned our posts the word soon got out that the sound and sonar equipment operator had picked up an unidentified submarine on our tail. After about two hours of being on pins and needles, the unidentified craft backed off. The best we could figure is that it was a German submarine that must have thought our ship was too small. That was just fine with us. I thought our ship was a little small for a naval vessel at first, but after this experience I thought that maybe that would work to our advantage.

As we continued our northern course we made a couple of stops before our first real test of rough seas. Cape Hatteris lived up to its history of being a very rough ocean. As I thought about this now, I thought of it more as a drill to prepare us for this typhoon that put us in our precarious position, but Cape Hatteris did not compare to the seventy-foot waves and 120 mile per hour winds that blew us through the air like leaves. How I wished we were still in Cape Hatteris. I would have happily given up my raft ride to be floating in the Cape with just my life vest. In comparison, it would have been at least a thousand times easier.

I will never forget the thrill of seeing the Statue of Liberty for the first time as we passed Ellis Island on our way to Staten Island. Staten Island was going to be our home base. I had only seen the Statue in pictures prior to this day and it was much more surreal seeing it in person than seeing it in pictures. I stood in awe of this giant statue and all that it stood for – liberty, freedom, the pursuit of happiness. These were the very things I joined the military to help protect. Growing up during the Great Depression my family was financially poor, so I was never in a position to travel the country and visit all its wonderful sights. The military gave me my first opportunity, and the Statue of Liberty really was a beautiful sight to see for this poor boy from Orange, Texas. It was more exciting than I ever imagined it could be. The only thing missing at that time was my wife and son. If they were there it would have been a perfect experience.

For the next year we housed ourselves on Staten Island. From here we received our assignment. We would be in the North Atlantic minesweeping ahead of large convoys of ships headed for Europe. When they told us this would to be our job for the remainder of the war, I thought, 'We'll see.' After all, I thought I would be a naval fireman in Florida for the remainder of the war and that definitely did not happen.

Several other minesweepers would meet with our ship just outside New York harbor and together we would lead a convoy of supply ships east through the treacherous waters of the Atlantic for several days. At our turning point we would meet a returning convoy and lead them back to the United States along the same path. Sticking to the same path tended to keep the mine sweeping easier, because once we cleaned out the mines, it would be a little more difficult for the Germans to lay mines in the same area.

On several occasions we did the mine sweeping for the Queen Mary as she transported troops between the U.S. and Europe. Going back and forth like this was our assignment for that entire year. It was dangerous, but our crew gained experience and we were good at it.

The German wolf packs were laying mines in the path of our supply ships that were headed out to supply our W.W.II fighting forces. There were three types of mines they were dropping. One type was an acoustical mine. When they picked up the sound from any passing ship, they would activate, arm themselves and rise to the surface in an attempt to strike the bottom of the passing ship. If the mine happened to miss its target, it would float around on the surface waiting for a passing ship to run into it. Another type was a magnetic mine. A magnetic mine would wait under water until a steel hull ship would pass overhead, then it would activate in an attempt to strike the bottom of the passing ship. Our ship was safe from this type of mine because we had a wood bottom. However, we did have equipment that would trigger these mines and bring them to the surface so we could destroy them. The third type was a contact mine. This mine just floated around on the surface hoping a passing ship would run into it. These were most effective at night because they were nearly impossible to see. During the day they were much easier to spot, but they still caused a great deal of damage to many ships.

During this year in the North Atlantic we were given the opportunity to train a group of Russian Navy personnel on how to perform all the different skills on mine warfare. We taught them how to bring the mines to the surface, then we taught them how to destroy the mines. In addition to that we had to teach them how to use depth charges in order to protect themselves from German wolf packs.

One day while we were patrolling for mines our sonar operator heard a German submarine very close to us. He gave us a bead on its approximate location and we launched several depth charges in that direction. About thirty seconds after one of the charges went off, we noticed a large oil slick come to the surface with clothing mixed in with it. We never saw any bodies or equipment, but we were all very certain we had just sunk a German submarine. Shortly there after, we proceeded with our patrolling. It felt kind of good to know that we stopped a submarine that probably already sank many ships in the American convoys.

The North Atlantic was a very rough and cold place. There were times when we would return to our home base and our ship looked like one big chunk of ice. As our ship would hit the on coming waves, the water would freeze and build up with each splash. Of course this would happen only during the winter. We would have to remove some of these chunks just so we could walk around easier. Sometimes they were so big they would actually block our walking paths.

On one of our returns to the New York harbor, we entered one of the worst fog layers I had ever seen. The skipper placed a look out at the bow and the stern of our ship to look for other ships at anchor in the harbor. All of a sudden a giant ship appeared before us through the fog. The bows look out, in an attempt to avoid a collision, yelled out, "Full speed astern!" Our ship's forward motion stopped and we began to go in reverse. A short moment later the sterns look out yelled, "Look out, full speed ahead!" The next thing that came was a loud crunching noise as the anchor chain from another big ship began cutting through the ribs of our ship. This unavoidable collision put us in the dry dock repair for over a month, and the skipper gave all of us a thirty-day leave. Thank God for small accidents. I now had thirty days to go be with my family.

I was excited about going home to see my wife and son and the rest of my family. When I asked how to get back to California for my thirty-day leave, I was told to go to the air base in New Jersey and pay one dollar for the use of a parachute. They were going to fly me all the way to the west coast. Anxious to get home quick, I made my way to the U.S. Air Base, and I was in the air that same morning.

What I thought would be a quick flight home turned out to be quite a fiasco. As we headed west in bad weather, we were ordered down in Harrisburg Pennsylvania due to the brunt of a winter snowstorm closing in on us. After one night on the ground our pilot, who happened to be Mac Arthur's personal pilot, convinced the officer in charge to let us go because of a rigid schedule the pilot had to meet. We were cleared and off we went down the east coast, only to be grounded in Mobile, Alabama due to an engine problem. We spent the night there while the engine was worked on over night. The next morning we were on our way again only to be forced down in Fort Worth, Texas because of bad weather. At this point I decided I would buy a train ticket to Los Angeles from Fort Worth. The train ride from Fort Worth to El Paso was eating up my leave time, so when the train stopped in El Paso I called the U.S. Air Base there and was told to take a taxi cab and rush out to the base and pay another dollar for a parachute. The plane was ready to take off and head to Los Angeles. I made the flight, and after a couple of hours in the air I was finally with my family. Sometimes the speed of the military is not so speedy.

It was great to see everybody again. My wife never looked more beautiful to me, and my son was a pleasure to hold. Seeing the rest of my family was also a delightful familiarity. Together, we all had a wonderful time and together we all went to church. Church was very important to all of us and we were all very thankful for our Christian heritage. Unfortunately, my leave seemed to go by in the blink of an eye. Before I knew it I had to head back to New York City. Once again, heart broken and begrudgingly, I left my family and made it back to New York City. Unlike the trip home, my trip back was very quick and without incident. Wasn't that ironic!

As I thought back about my time around New York City, the big apple really knew how to entertain our service men. I arrived back one day early from my leave and I went to the USO. They told me that the Salvation Army would check me in for lodging and meals at no cost to me. It was quite a reception. I was given tickets to Broadway productions and radio broadcasts. It was exciting to watch Perry Como broadcast his first radio appearance. Along with about ten other service men it was nice being a part of Fred Waring's orchestra. We sat with them at a banquet, and also sat in on their live broadcast from New York City. The USO sure knew how to show us military guys a real good time. It was a great experience, and I could have stayed there the remainder of the war.

On one occasion I was pulled out of line at the Bob Hawk, "Thanks to the Yanks" broadcast and was told I would be one of the contestants on the radio show. When the show was complete, I won a case of 15,000 Camel cigarettes. Since I was not a smoker, I took advantage of my good fortune and I sold all the cigarettes to various smokers for seventy-five dollars. That was a large amount of money for that time and it was just the right amount of money to purchase myself a brand new, tailor made uniform. It was a uniform I wore with pride. Oh how I wished I were back in New York City at this time.

I was taken out of my memory tree when I felt somebody squeezing my leg. When I opened my eyes I saw Joe Mendello grabbing my leg again asking me if I would give him a Pepsi that was inside my leg. His behavior was deteriorating and there was nothing we could do. He just took in far too much seawater. Once again I assured him that it was not a Pepsi by lifting my pant leg and showing him that it really was my leg. He stopped asking, but I do not think he completely believed me. He just leaned his back against the side of the raft, tilted his head back, closed his eyes and quietly mumbled to himself. I could tell he was having one heck of a time trying to keep his wits about himself. I could also see that if we did not get help soon, he was not going to last too much longer. All I could do is pray, hope for the best and wait.

Things began to turn from bad to worse on day four. The sun bore down on us with no protection and the parts of our skin that were exposed to the sun were now black. I was extremely tired, but my level of fatigue was dwarfed in comparison to my level of thirst. My skin hurt from the morbid sunburn, and the saltwater ulcers were a painfully, persistent nuisance. My cracked lips were getting worse. My parched mouth was hopelessly waterless, and my dry throat was taking my voice. I did not want to talk in order to preserve what little energy I had left, and even if I wanted to I do not think I would have been able to do so very easily anyway.

As I looked across the raft, I noticed that two of my buddies, Mark Hartman and Freeman Hetzer, were carrying on a very quiet and secretive conversation. They spoke quietly for several minutes before they stopped and looked at the rest of us. When their conversation was finished Hartman spoke up and said that they both decided they were going to leave the raft and try to get some help by swimming to the island we could see off in the distance. It was my feeling that we were still twenty-five to thirty miles away from the peak of the mountain that we could still see. Fortunately, the peak was still visible on day four, but we knew it was quite a distance. We tried our best to talk them out of it by sternly reminding them of the shark-infested waters. We could see the sharks continuously swimming around our raft any time we looked overboard. However, they decided they had to take their chances and do it any way. They said, "If we stay here, we're just going to die in the raft. We have to at least try something." With that, Hartman slipped off his pants and just wore his briefs. Hetzer left his pants on and they both slipped into the water and started swimming away. Both men were wearing their life jackets. Hartman took the lead and Hetzer followed close behind. The seven of us still on the raft kept a close eye on them. When the two were about thirty or forty feet from the raft, Hartman suddenly yelled out with a horrid scream. About that same time Hetzer turned around and started swimming back toward the raft. At first we were not sure what was happening. It took a few seconds to figure out what was going on. But once we saw the thrashing water around Hartman begin to bubble with blood, we instantly knew it was a shark attack. In a panic, the rest of us jumped up and began to paddle in their direction with our hands. When we reached Hetzer we were able to pull him back into the raft, but when we looked up we noticed a very large pool of blood around Hartman's body, and he was no longer thrashing. He only yelled once and that was it. He did not yell anymore, as he floated on the surface in a puddle of blood that mixed with the seawater. In a state of confusion and shock, we all stared in disbelief as we watched the sharks come back and pull his limp body under the water and out of sight. Instinctively, at this point, we paddled away from him as fast as we could. There was so much blood in the water that we were in fear of the blood touching the raft and having the sharks mistake the raft for a person and begin attacking it. Frantically we paddled away from the point of the attack. Hetzer, who was right next to the attack when it occurred, was now on the raft with us. He was helping us paddle as well. We kept looking back at the point of the attack hoping to see some sign of life, but we saw nothing. We continued to anxiously paddle as we kept looking back hoping to see Hartman come to the surface and begin swimming toward us. We paddled until we thought we were far enough away from the pool of blood and out of harms way. We waited for a while looking in the direction of the attack in hopes of seeing Hartman. However, Hartman never resurfaced and we never saw him again. We were all incredibly shocked at what just happened and we were having a hard time believing it was real. This type of thing does not happen in real life. It only happens in stories conjured up from someone's imagination. The whole attack happened so fast that when it was over I had to stop and run the scenario through my head a few more times only to try and figure out what just took place. Being as worn out as I was, and on the verge of hallucination, I had to really think it through to realize that what occurred was actually real. I honestly felt like I was dreaming. But, as enough time passed and we began to settle down, we were beginning to realize that the nightmare we just witnessed was actually reality. It was truly unbelievable.

I was speechless even if I were able to talk. For the rest of that day we did not speak. We just sat there somberly in disbelief. We were all very scared at this point and wondered when the sharks would come back to get the rest of us. The fear and the heartache I was experiencing was almost debilitating. I felt like I wanted to collapse and just disappear, but I knew all I could really do was just sit there and wait, while I replayed the memory of that horrid shark attack over and over inside my head. I could not believe that Hartman was no longer with us. He was such a young man, I though, too young to die at this age. I wondered if there would be anymore of us leaving for good anytime soon. Hartman was the cook on board ship and I was beginning to have these mental images of him on the ship when we were on board together. It was a very interesting experience to actually see these images of him flash through my head of some of the experiences we had together on the ship. Nothing like this had ever happened to me before. All I could do is pass it off as shock, heartache and the hallucinations that were trying to haunt me.

As the sun began to set on the horizon at the end of the fourth day, I realized we were entering our fifth night on the raft. I was extremely tired, but my level of fatigue was dwarfed in comparison to my level of thirst. My skin hurt from the nearly morbid sunburn, and the saltwater ulcers were a painfully, persistent severe irritation. In addition to all this physical pain I was experiencing, I had to endure an intense level of emotional pain now that our number of sailors was down by one. Up to this point thoughts of death had not entered my mind, but after the shark attack I could not help but think of who would be next, or would we be rescued before one more of us fell.

Day 5

Chapter 5

As night fell on the fifth night, my shipmates were either very still or sleeping. All I could do at this point was go back to my memory tree. Having the circumstances as they were, and losing Hartman earlier in the day, made it increasingly difficult to achieve this task. My ability to focus was becoming laborious, but I forced myself to do it anyway. The punishment from our situation was beating me down and in addition to everything else I was also beginning to feel what I think people called "depression." Every time I would feel hopelessness and believe it was real the next thing that would follow was depression. I had to keep telling myself that hopelessness was just a thought and if I gave it any credit it would eventually win out in the form of depression. Once again I had to force myself to quit thinking about the negative by remembering all the positive events in my life. At this point I went back to my memory tree and thought back to when the war was over in Europe. We were ordered to head out to the south pacific to deal with the Japanese. We headed down the east coast and through the Panama Canal, and then we headed up the west cost to Newport, California to take on additional equipment. Our skipper, a very generous man, allowed me and a few of my fellow shipmates to spend most of our California time at my home in Whittier, which was only an hour drive from the ship. We were there for approximately one month. One beautiful month! It was one more month I was able to spend with my wife and my baby boy Richard. I was grateful that the war in Europe was over. We were not sure what was going to happen in the Pacific, but we were hopeful it would soon be over there as well. Japan was being so intensely bombed at the time that we knew they could not take it much longer, or at least we hoped they could not take it much longer. Eventually the orders came and it was time to ship out.

After taking on all our additional equipment, we headed out to sea. Our final destination was Okinawa Island. It was there that we were supposed to prepare for the invasion of Japan. Our first stop was Pearl Harbor. From Pearl Harbor we were supposed to re-supply, then head to Eniwetok, then to Saipan and finally Okinawa. We were half way between California and Pearl Harbor when we received word that Japan might be surrendering soon because they dropped this thing called the "atomic bomb" on Hiroshima, Japan. We did not know exactly what it was, but it sounded like it could bring a speedy end to this very ugly war. With this news, we were all extremely hopeful that it would be over sooner rather than later. I kept my fingers crossed that I would be going home sooner than I imagined.

We finally arrived in Pearl Harbor on August 13, 1945. There were hopeful people everywhere, both military and civilian. All the lights in the city were on and people were celebrating everywhere. Ships were firing tracers in the air and aiming them out to sea. They seemed to think the war would be over soon. By this time, America had dropped two atomic bombs on Japan that seemed to bring Japan to its knees. Our orders were to re-supply and prepare to head out to our final destination, Okinawa Island. It was the next day, August 14, that we received word Japan had officially surrendered. Renner and I took a trip into town. There was excitement everywhere. Soldiers were swapping uniforms as a joke and one soldier put on quite a strip tease for an audience in the street. The whole town was in a mad frenzy of excitement. It could not have been a better day for the war to end, because August 14, 1945 was also my anniversary. Three years to the day Ida and I were married. What a day to end the war. Boy was I happy. After the festivities I found time to write Ida a letter. This would turn out to be the last letter I sent home before we were sunk.

Aug 14, 1945
My darling wife and son;
The war is over and I don't have to tell you how happy I am. Yes darling today is the big day. O'boy that means a lot to me. First because it is our anniversary, and second, the war has ended today. I am sorry I was unable to send you a card and a giftt. I hope you did as I said and spent $30 on yourself for clothing. Be sure and do that honey and I will send it to you out of my pay.

I went into Honolulu today just to see the parade and excitement. All the stores were closed and the town was full of people. Soldiers were exchanging clothes with soldiers. One seaman had a Commander's hat on. We saw one striptease and the whole town was a mad house.

Renner and I went in together and we watched the crowd of people for three hours and then we went to Hotel Yong for dinner. It is an American Hotel, the Langls & Swarnkhiest bldg. in Honolulu. We then went back on the streets and saw fireworks and a display of colored lights. We decided to come back to the ship before the crowd went completely mad, so we were waiting for a bus and a soldier and a Lt came by in a jeep and said they would take us out to the base and they brought us right up to the ship. It was sure nice of them.

Yes angel, three years ago today you changed your name from Ida Mae Campbell to Mrs. H.R. Harrison. You are all mine and I am very proud of you. You're perfect disposition, your cute smile, your cute figure. Well you're just cute.

I love you very much and I'll get home just as fast as I can, so keep the home frills beckoning and save all you can.

> *Yours always*
> *Your loving Husband*
> *Bill.*

We were supposed to head out to Okinawa to prepare for the invasion of Japan. But, thanks to the atomic bomb, the invasion of Japan was never going to take place. We were all ecstatic and very happy about this news. We had our own celebration out at sea, and everyone's smile seemed to be stretched from ear to ear. We really did not have anything else to celebrate with except our smiles. The joy of no more war was quite the euphoric experience. Many of my shipmates and I were talking about what we were going to do when we finally made it home. We spoke of family, friends and future plans. The excitement on the ship was electrifying. I almost forgot what it was like to live in peace, but the reality of it came flooding back into my life again and it was an absolute gorgeous experience. I never knew I could feel so perfect in my life now that I had a wonderful wife and a beautiful newborn son. The only thing left to be done was to finish my Naval duties and make it home to begin my new life without the interruption of war.

Our new orders came in and we were instructed to head out to Okinawa anyway and help clear the way to lead occupational troops into Japan. The concept of clearing the water without the threat of an enemy was an unfamiliar notion to me, but nonetheless, it was very appreciated. As far as I knew, there was no danger and as soon as our job was complete we would be going home permanently.

By knowing the war was over, I had some time to ponder. As I looked back over my three years and two months in the Navy, I realized that traveling between different schools, home leave and delays; I had crossed the United States thirteen times. That adds up to about 39,000 miles of travel, and that did not include all the miles I put in out at sea. That was just the miles traveled over land, and it was a huge chunk of traveling for a homebody like myself.

We made it to Eniwetok, re-supplied and fueled up. From there we headed out to Saipan. When we arrived at Saipan Captain Blaser gave us about six hours of shore leave. We gladly accepted it. As we walked around the island and on the beach we kept hearing consistent, but sporadic machine gun fire. About every five seconds I would hear the burst of a machine gun – first behind me, then off to my right, then behind me again, then off to my left. I heard it come from much higher up on the hill at the center of the island. It never stopped and it was actually making me pretty nervous and tense. I could not figure out what they were doing. When I saw a Marine pass buy I asked him what was happening. He told me there were still Japanese on the island who did not know the war was over, so they kept on fighting. The Marines were still mopping up all these hot spots. The Marine also told me that the Japs kept sneaking into the mess hall and stealing food on a regular basis. He said it did not sound like a big deal, but it was becoming a big problem. They were stealing a lot of food. It was nice to have my feet on land for a short while, but I could not wait to get off of that island and back on our ship. With all that gunfire I did not feel safe at all.

When we finally arrived in Okinawa, my shipmates and I felt a little spooked about the number thirteen that kept appearing. Upon leaving the west coast our ship's number, YMS 472, added up to thirteen. Our sister ship 454 along with two other ships, the 292 and the 346 all added up to thirteen. We arrived in Pearl Harbor on August the thirteenth and the day we arrived in Okinawa it was September the thirteenth. Three days later, our ship went down in that nasty typhoon. I am not superstitious, but that was one heck of a coincidence, I think. Or was it really just a foreshadow of what awaited us?

As I opened my eyes, the night was turning into twilight. It was the beginning of day five. I kept my eyes closed and head tilted forward until the sun began to peek over the horizon. At this point, the intensity of my thirst was enormous. I had no idea that thirst could be so physically painful. I was so thirsty that it actually hurt. God, how I wished I had just one glass of water. The more I thought about it the more excruciating it seemed to be, so I had to force myself to ignore it. As I looked around at each one of my shipmates my questioning thought was, "Who would be next and what event would cause his death?" I had a feeling things would not go well today.

It was on this day that we all agreed not to talk about anything that was water or food related. The thought of these basic necessities, without being able to possess them, only intensified the torture we were already experiencing. We were not interested in inflicting ourselves with any more pain than we were already enduring. It was definite. We would not talk about any more food or water from this point on.

As the hot sun began to take its toll, Joe Mendello continued to accuse me of hiding a bottle of Pepsi Cola from him. He grabbed my calf through my pants and said, " I know you're hiding a can of soda in there, why don't you take it out and share it with me?" I assured him it was not soda, but it was my calf. On this day it was impossible to convince him that it actually was my calf muscle and not a soda can underneath my pants. He was hallucinating pretty badly. It took me the better part of an hour to get him to calm down and believe it was really my leg. He also would not stop scooping up the salt water and drinking it. We had to take turns having our arms and legs wrapped around him in order to keep him from drinking the deadly brine.

Mendello finally settled down and we convinced him not to drink any more seawater. While he sat there in a relaxed mode for a short while, he began to speak out loud to another shipmate, Freeman Hetzer. He said to Freeman, "My father was killed in a coal mining accident, my brother was killed in Germany, and if this kills me it will kill my mother." We all sat there in a stunned silence just starring at him. We were not sure how to respond to that. We could not exactly tell him that everything was going to be just fine because things were horrible and growing worse by the minute. We lost Hartman the day before and Mendello had filled himself with saltwater. The silence that filled the raft at that moment was almost deafening. The thought of his mother dying over losing her whole family was emotionally crushing to say the least. If we had any tears left in our tear ducts we all would have cried at that moment, but we could not. We just told him to not give up hope. As long as we were alive, there was a chance for rescue. He did not seem very hopeful no matter what we said. It looked to me like he was giving up. Mendello was the baby of the family and my heart just ached for his poor mother. All we could do is hope to God that Mendello would not give up and fight on until we were rescued. That was all we could do for his sake and his mother's.

We decided to make one more attempt at making to the island we could see off in the distance, but this time we decided to cut the webbed flooring off of the raft with a knife that Wayne Neyland had with him. We thought that maybe the flooring was causing too much drag for the raft to move swiftly through the water. After cutting it off we all began paddling toward the island. It seemed like we were paddling forever when we realized that we were making absolutely no progress. So, we stopped. Now without our webbed flooring all we had to sit on was the rim of the raft. It was only nine inches wide and very uncomfortable.

For the rest of that morning we sat quiet and motionless on the rim as the sun beat down on us. We did this until the sun was about at the peak of its arc. It was about noon when Wayne B. Neyland, decided he wanted to leave the raft. At that time I was the only one that had a dry life jacket. I had folded up the bottom portion of it to prevent it from becoming water soaked. It seemed that the raft was soaking up water and it looked like it was sitting a little lower in the ocean everyday. I knew by keeping my jacket dry it would hold me up in the water another seventy-two hours. Neyland was asking for my life jacket being that it was not water logged. I was afraid I might need it later, and I did not want to give it up, but after about an hour of hearing his reasoning, I felt his request was just another option for our possible rescue. Apprehensively, I handed him my life jacket. He put it on and said, "If we're going to die out here we have to at least try something." As he slipped into the water, we all warned him about the sharks. Our eyes were fixed on him as he began to swim off. When he was about the same distance Hartman was when he was attacked by the sharks, nothing happened. He just kept swimming. We were all just waiting for him to get hit by a shark. We watched him move up and down on the swells until he was out of sight. Unfortunately, no help ever came from that area.

Our man count was now down to seven. In addition to losing two men from the raft, we had to continue to take turns holding our arms around Mendello and now Ted Cullanan. They were both scooping up the seawater and drinking it. Ted Cullanan kept jumping in the water and swimming around the raft mumbling nonsense to him self. We kept pulling him back in and telling him to relax in the raft. No sooner would we tell him to relax when he would jump back in the water, and swim around the raft mumbling nonsense again. Freeman Hetzer pulled him in one time and said, "You need to settle down or you're going to fall off and the sharks are going to kill you like they killed Hartman." Cullanan finally did settle down for a short while.

Less than an hour after we had Cullanan settle down, and several hours after Neyland left with my life jacket, Joe Mendello began to speak like he was completely out of his mind. He kept saying over and over, "I am going to get a taxi to go home and if anyone wants to go with me I will pay your way. I have plenty of money so you guys don't have to worry about it. It's my treat." We were very worried for him and all we could do is wrap our arms and legs around him in an attempt to keep him from drinking any more seawater. We kept telling him to settle down and that everything would be okay, but at this point he seemed to have completely lost control of his mind. I am not even sure he knew what was going on at that time. His eyes may have been open and his mouth talking, but I tend to think he was completely unconscious. It was quite a sad sight to see. I could not help but think of his mother. I also could not help thinking that the rest of us were not very far behind him. I personally was not sure how much longer I would be able to hang onto what little sanity I had left. Mendello was being held by Bob Hicks when it happened. Suddenly, Mendello, in a twisting motion turned in order to break Bob Hicks grasp on him. He then stood up on the edge of the raft and did a belly flop in the ocean. Frantically, he started swimming as fast as he could while he was yelling at the top of his lungs for the taxi to stop. We were yelling for him to come back, but there was absolutely no chance of him hearing our calls. We watched him swim away until we could no longer see him or hear him. He was so out of his mind that he was not even swimming in the direction of the island we could see. He actually swam in the opposite direction. The salt water and the five-day ordeal finally wore him down.

Our number was down to six on this day. As I sat there pondering in shock and disbelief, I noticed that the first boy to leave the raft took his pants off because he did not want to carry any extra weight. I think the shark attacked him due to his white skin possibly getting the sharks attention.

Sharks did not attack Freeman Hetzer. They also did not seem to attack Wayne Neyland or Joe Mendello as far as I could tell. They were all wearing their pants. Two were able to swim out of sight and sound. One was right next to Hartman when they attacked and they did not bother him. Hartman did not get much more than thirty feet when he was attacked. The best I could guess is that the color of the Navy dungarees did not attract the shark's curiosity as much as the color of flesh.

We were all in sad shape at this point. I was having a hard time separating hallucination from reality. I would see many ships at one time near to us, then I would blink my eyes and they would all be gone. They sure looked real. I was also seeing blimps all over the sky with chains hanging off the bottom of them. They would come down low as if they were going to pick us up, then I would blink my eyes again and they would all disappear. If somebody said something or described something, I could see it. It was amazing to see how my mind was playing such vivid tricks on me. Whatever was said, I could see it. This was not just happening to me. It was happening to other guys as well. At this point, we decided not to talk about anything so we would not confuse each other. We were all at the point of not being able to distinguish between reality and hallucination.

Later on in the afternoon, I guessed it to be around 3:00 p.m., due to the position of the sun, one of my closest shipmates, Norman Plumb, began to look down in the water. As he was looking down, he started saying, "Bill, I can see the ship down there. I am going down below to get some pineapple juice that I hid in the engine room. There was a half a case left. Look, you can see our ship sunk right below us." When I looked over the side I could see everything he described. I could see the ship under the water with lights on and sailors walking on the deck. We were both convinced that what we were seeing was real. At this point I should have realized that I was starting to fade fast, but I honestly could not tell the difference between reality and hallucination. So, instead of telling Norman not to go down there and that it was just a hallucination, I encouraged him by saying, "Well, if you think you know where the juice is, then go down there and bring it up. We can all use some." Then I asked him, "Are you sure you want to do this with all those sharks in the water?" He insisted that he do it. He also said he would be right back with the pineapple juice. With that, I told him to be careful. In the next moment, I watched my best Naval buddy slip over the side of the raft and swim down toward our hallucination. I watched him swim out of sight, and then waited for him to return with the pineapple juice. I kept telling myself, 'Any second now he should be coming up.' He never came back up, and we never saw him again. We waited about two hours before we realized he was never coming back. I do not know if the sharks grabbed him or if he just went so far down that he was unable to make it to the surface to catch his next breath. The only thing I did know is that he did not resurface anywhere around us.

When the magnitude of what happened finally reached my clouded mind, I felt terrible for letting him go. If only I could have kept my mind clear I would never have let him go down. It was heartbreaking to know that I just watch my best friend literally swim to his death. Looking back, I know the sun bearing down on us for five days while we had no protection, no food and no water was really beginning to take its toll. We were all beginning to see these things that made no sense and there was nothing we could do about it, but that did not make it any easier when we would lose a friend. I was completely heartbroken and sick to my stomach after this event. I cried after this happened, yet, I was too dehydrated to shed tears.

When the sun finally set signaling the end of day five there were only five of the original nine left. There was Bob Hicks, Freeman Hetzer, Elmer Renner, Ted Cullanan and myself. We were physically depleted and emotionally drained. Ted Cullanan kept jumping in the water and swimming around the raft while he was mumbling nonsense. We kept talking him back into the raft, but there came a point when there was nothing we could do but ask him to get back in. After a few requests he would get back in. The last thing I remember on that fifth night shortly before I went to sleep was Ted Cullanan in the water swimming around the edge of the raft talking to himself. He was pulled in by the other guys and reminded of the sharks. He would settle down. We would close our eyes for just a few seconds, and he would jump right back in the water only to be pulled back in the raft. I myself was too tired to help anymore so I closed my eyes and went to sleep. Even though it was difficult to sleep on the rim of the raft, my fatigue over took me and I fell asleep anyway.

When I woke up the next morning to start day six of our nightmarish, nasty ordeal, Ted Cullanan was nowhere to be seen. None of us saw where he went or what happened to him. We only knew that when we woke up that morning he was gone. There was no sign of him in the water, no sign of him on the horizon and no sound from him anywhere. He just disappeared. As gone as our minds were at the time, we thought that maybe he might come back, but he never did. The only thing we concluded was that he probably ended up swimming away in a similar fashion to Joe Mendello.

With only four of us left we began to wonder once again who would be next and what would cause the problem. I wondered when it would be my turn and what the circumstances would be. Would it be quick, easy and painless or would it be a rough experience? Was it going to hurt or would it be okay?

Day six was by far the hottest of all the days. Usually there were some high clouds that would offer us a momentary reprieve through the glistening day, but on this date there was not a single cloud in the sky. The unforgiving sun just pounded the remaining four of us on this day. Our skin was black, our bodies hurt and our minds were almost gone. As the day wore on, the baking sun began to do its thing. Our thinking started crazy visions of senseless patterns of wacky images and things we had made a rule not to talk about – water or food. I was very careful in trying to explain the drinking fountain I saw floating through the air. It had a frosted turn on button gray in color. I fought the urge as long as I could, but this hallucination was so vivid that I could not hold my tongue any longer. I asked Freeman Hetzer if he could see the drinking fountain that was floating toward me from the sky. After I described it to him he said, "I see the gray housing but tell me again, which side is the Westinghouse label on?" It would float toward me in the air, and then back away. The longer I kept my eyes opened the more details I could see. Then, in the blink of an eye, it vanished. Again, I saw a blimp in the sky with chains hanging from it. It would come in close as if it was going to pick us up with the chain, then I would close my eyes and open them and the blimp would disappear. These hallucinations were like being conscious and having very vivid dreams while my eyes were open.

With the exception of describing our hallucinations, we remained quiet for the first half of that day. Based on the position of the sun, it was around noontime when Bob Hicks began to talk. He said, "I feel like I'll be next to die, and if I do not feed the sharks you can have my body." After his statement, we all looked at each other for a moment. We were not sure how to respond to that announcement. We all looked around at each other as if we were not sure what we just heard, but the look on everybody's face just confirmed that what we heard was accurate. This statement should have shocked us, but so many devastating things had been happening in the last two days that nothing was surprising anymore. After just a few moments of contemplation, we understood what he was saying and then we all agreed to the same idea. We gave each other permission to eat our body if we died. We decided that if it would help some of us get rescued then it was worth the sacrifice.

Our thirst was much stronger than our hunger, but our hunger was beginning to intensify. I lost my hunger drive on the second day, but a couple days later it came back with strength. As we looked over the side of the raft, we could see a school of small fish fifteen or twenty feet below the surface. So, we all tore off about four inches from the bottom part of our shirts, then tore those into about one inch strips. We tied them together making one long strip. We dangled this cloth into the water toward the school of fish hoping they would bite at it and maybe get their teeth caught in the cloth. Then, we would pull them in and eat them. However, the fish were not interested. We tried this for about an hour before we gave up.

As the hunger intensified on this day, one boy sitting across from me started to stare at my midsection. I thought, 'Hold on. Wait a minute. I'm not dead yet.' He then slid across the raft and grabbed my leather belt, unbuckled it, pulled it out and started chewing on one end. I thought, 'Hey, that's my belt so if there is any nutritional value in it then it is mine more than yours.' So, I started chewing on the other end. It didn't take long to determine it was only imitation leather. It had a very bad taste and it began to come apart in our mouths. Needless to say, we had to spit the stuff out.

I was becoming so desperate that I tried to eat the wood floats on the side of the raft. My thoughts were that this wood came from a tree. It had sap and moisture running through it at one time and just maybe there was some sap moisture still in it. I began to chew on it and instead of finding any moisture I ended up with a mouth full of salty splinters. I gave up my quest for food and water at this point, so I just sat there.

We sat silent until the sun was getting low on the horizon. Another day was coming to an end, and we were still lost. I honestly thought we would have been rescued by now, but begrudgingly we were not. And, about two hours before dark, I began to realize something. In a moment of mental and emotional stillness, I began to realize the unthinkable. In my mind I could actually see that I was not going to survive through the seventh night. I am not sure how I knew this, but it was certain. It was definite, and it was a very unfamiliar experience. I really had not even begun to live my life like I hoped and planned, and now it was already coming to an end before I was given the chance to genuinely live it to the fullest. It was not fair, I thought, and all I could think at this point is that, "I'm going to die." I almost could not believe this was really happening. What would it be like? Would it hurt? Would it be painless? Would it be scary? Would it be peaceful? I did not know the answer to these questions. I only knew that at the dawn of day seven, I would not be alive. It was an extremely weird concept. I did not want this to happen, but there was nothing I could do, there was nothing I could say and there was nothing I could make happen to change my misfortune. I could only see this strict reality before me. I knew it was my time to leave my body. God was calling me home. God was calling me home. That was all I could think for the next few moments, God was calling me home. The more I thought this, the more I repeated it. The more I repeated it, the more I felt like I was being consumed by a peaceful veil of acceptance that I had never experienced before this moment. It seemed like a deeper part of me knew that if it were my time to go home to heaven then everything would be just fine. It was as if suddenly I had nothing to fret over any longer. I began to think back on my years and remember what a good life I had. I thought about my childhood and my teenage years. I thought about my good military experiences with my good buddies. Then I started to think of my wife Ida, my son Richard, my mother and my father back in Whittier, California. I could only hope that the news of my death would not be too difficult on them. I loved them all far too much to want them to fret over me leaving this earth. All these thoughts went through my head real fast as if they were being projected from a film reel. Once again I began to thank God for my Christian heritage and what a good life God had given me up to this point. I really had nothing to complain about. I had a short, but beautiful life. I was grateful to have the short time I was given than to not have any time at all. Five minutes with Ida and Richard would have been better than no time at all. I was given much more than that. I thanked God for my wonderful family and I knew they were praying for my rescue at this time. I thanked God for every experience that was ever given to me and I appreciated every second of my life that had already passed. I thanked God over and over. I must have thanked God for ten straight minutes without stopping, and when I was done thanking God, I was at perfect peace with my circumstances, my destiny and myself. I had given every day my best and there was nothing else I could do. Even on the days where I might have fallen short, they were the best I could do at that time. I knew I always gave everyday my best and I felt good about that. I was ready to die and I knew everything was going to be okay when I made it home to heaven. I relaxed and seemed to enter an unfamiliar altered state of true peace. I was perfectly comfortable and calm under these dire circumstances. It was strange. I thought it was just God's way of preparing me for my crossing-over experience. I was at peace and I was ready. So I sat quiet, still and waited for it to overtake me. While I was in this tranquil state, I began to look toward the mountain peak that we had tried so many times to reach. We could see safety, yet safety could not see us. This peak made rescue seem so close and yet so far. It was still some twenty-five to thirty miles away and we were never going to make it there. I focused my gaze on the peak and stared at it. As I was staring at the peak a thought entered my mind. It was a memory thought that reminded me of a scripture in the Bible that my mother would read to us kids just before we would leave for school – MATTHEW 17:20 – "If you have faith as small as a mustard seed God can remove a mountain." I repeated this verse in my head one more time "If you have faith as small as a mustard seed God can remove a mountain" then I repeated it again and again. There was something about the verse that seemed to activate something deep within myself that was triggering a familiar but distant idea. I could not quite pinpoint it so I kept repeating it over and over and over. Every time I would say it, it was as if a little spark would fire up inside me. The more I said it the more the spark would fire. The more the spark would fire the longer it would glow. Eventually the glow began to burn. When the burn erupted into a raging fire the answer finally hit me! I realized up to this point on the raft that after the conclusion of all my prayers I would immediately have unpleasant and negative thoughts about the Navy not sending help to rescue us. I could suddenly see that I was not praying in faith and faith had not at all been a part of my prayers. "My prayers had no faith!" I thought. "They were empty shells devoid of substance. They were useless nothings, and, thus far, all my prayers had been a waste of time." It was at this moment the true meaning of faith revealed itself to me. It was as if a veil had been removed from before the eyes in my mind, and, out of the blue, I could see. I suddenly knew that true faith had nothing to do with empty prayer. True faith was simply thanking God for the answer before it gets there, and knowing the answer is coming. "Thanking God for the answer before it gets there and knowing the answer is coming," I thought. With that in mind I looked at my shipmates. They were all sitting down slumped over on the rim of the raft, some with their knees up and others with their feet and legs submerged in the water. Their foreheads were resting against their knees, or their cheeks were resting against the palms of their hands and their eyes were closed. Elmer Renner had been in this position the longest. When we would call him he would not always respond to our cries. He had been this way since day three. He was just sitting there in his own little world.

After my epiphany I noticed the condition of my shipmates. I am sure this is where God gave me the words that I spoke. I do not know where the strength came from, but I started talking. The more I said, the more I noticed that Freeman Hetzer and Bob Hicks, who were sitting across from me, were leaning toward me to hear every word I had to say. Elmer Renner also began to come out of his exhausted state. I told the three of them that I completely forgot about the word faith in my prayers. I told them about my mother's Bible verse and that faith believes, and knows. And the best way to be faithful is to start thanking God for the answer to our prayers.

Bob Hicks asked me, "Now how do I get this faith?" I told him to follow me in my prayer and I said, "When you ask God to forgive you for anything you have done that was displeasing to Him promise Him that you will do all within your power to increase your faith in Him. When you're finished with your prayer, start thanking Him for the answer to your prayers." After my speech to him he began praying a simple prayer. When he was finished with his prayer he said, "Much obliged God." Freeman Hetzer began to pray and said, "God, if you're going to take me please just make it quick. I don't want to suffer. Amen."

When I concluded my prayer I must have thanked God sixty or more times. At this point Elmer Renner had come out of his own mind set and was much more alert and responsive then he had been. I started the four of us celebrating on board the raft by singing songs. We suddenly seemed to have strength that we thought was completely gone. At this point I had a very strong feeling that the button had been pushed for our rescue. We sang non-stop for about forty-five minutes. I knew we were going to be okay, I just did not know exactly how. It was an amazing feeling to know that we were going to be rescued regardless of our situation. It seemed impossible, but I believed and I knew it was going to happen. We sang and sang and sang. We sang loud and we did not want to stop. We all sang like we were alone and nobody was listening. Eventually, after nearly an hour of continuous singing, we had to stop to take a break. For some reason we all felt energized, excited and peaceful. If we died at this point, nobody ever would have believed that we were so jubilant in our last moments. But we were. Within just a few moments of our break, we could hear something. It sounded like airplanes. When we turned our heads in the direction of the sound we saw three planes lined up one behind the other. They were not coming in our direction. They were actually paralleling us as they headed toward the island that we could see. They must have been six or seven miles away and about five hundred feet off the surface of the ocean. We began waving our arms and yelling. I stood up on the corner of the raft that I was sitting in. Looking back over the heads of my shipmates who were sitting in front of me now, I took my white undershirt off and began waving it. Elmer Renner, who was still sitting, grabbed my hand to help balance me. The first of the three airplanes kept heading in the direction of the island. About a quarter mile behind him the second plane continued following the first plane and it was obvious that he also was heading to the island. About a quarter mile behind the second plane, the third plane was also heading toward the island when suddenly he made a left hand turn and began heading directly at us. He was six or seven miles away when he did this and I thought there is no way he could see us out here. The water was blue. The raft was gray-blue, and our clothes were gray-blue. As I stood waving, the plane continued on its course towards us. As he was drawing closer the raft began to turn in the water. Not wanting to change my position I stood waving with the plane behind me as Elmer held onto my hand. I was not sure if the plane was actually headed toward us because I could not turn around to see. So, I looked down at Elmer and watched his eyes. Elmer squirmed in his seat a little as his eyes began to open wide. Reading his body language I was becoming excited thinking the plane was still coming in our direction. A short moment later Elmer's eyes welled up with tears and he started crying. This was something I did not want to see, because his tears told me the plane was not coming in our direction anymore. Even though I continued waving, my heart plunged into my stomach and shattered into a million pieces. I was instantaneously heart broken, because Elmer's eyes told me the plane must have turned around. About five seconds later, Elmer's tears and crying turned into laughter. When he began laughing I knew the plane was drawing closer and could probably see us. I continued waving, and as I looked over my shoulder I saw the most beautiful airplane I had ever seen in my whole life. It was a Navy Blue United States Navy Corsair with bent wings near the fuselage, and, like an angel straight from heaven, it dipped its left wing about two hundred feet off the surface of the ocean and began circling us. All four of us burst into laughter and tears of the purest joy that could ever exist on the face of the earth. We all stood up laughing, crying and hugging each other. The other two planes turned around and joined the third plane circling us. Tears began to pour out of my eyes as I laughed with euphoria. I had no idea where these tears came from, but they were there. The pilot of the first plane that began circling us threw a package out that landed in the water near to us, but we were too weak to paddle to it. It looked like a first aid kit. Then, he dropped a smoke bomb to mark our position. The plane that was originally leading the first two planes to the island turned around and headed back toward the island. The other two planes just kept circling us. About twenty minutes later and about twenty minutes before dark, a Martin PBM Mariner twin-engine floatplane landed in the water a few hundred feet away. He slowly taxied over to our position and pulled up along side of us. A door opened on the side of the plane and an Air Sea Rescue sailor began to throw life preservers in our direction. One of the life preservers had a rope tied to it. We grabbed the rope and pulled ourselves toward the plane. When we were about three feet away, Freeman Hetzer jumped out of the raft and into the plane. After they pulled the raft up to the plane the rest of us were helped in. They kicked the raft away from the plane and immediately put us in bunk beds. While we were lying there the pilot turned around and told us that if it had been ten minutes later he would have had to abort the rescue until the following morning. When they put us down on the bunks, I knew it was for real and we were finally going home. With tears in my eyes, I thanked God almost non-stop for this incredible miracle. We were finally rescued!

Recovery

CHAPTER 6

It took only twenty minutes of flying time to reach the Hospital ship, the USS Pine Island at anchor off the coast of Okinawa. We were lifted up the side of the ship in stretchers by cables. I remembered seeing more sailors than I had ever seen before. They were all hanging over the side of the ship that we were being lifted onto. There were giant floodlights pointed at us with Naval personnel everywhere. They were curious to see the guys that spent six days on a raft with no food or water. There must have been a thousand eyeballs watching us be lifted on board that evening. Some of the looks on the faces were curious, some were anxious and worried looking, some were smiling, but to me, all of them were beautiful. That was without a doubt the finest looking group of sailors I had ever seen in my whole life.

Oh what a happy feeling it was to know we were going to get water, food and medical attention. We were placed in the medical ward where they hooked us up to an I.V. tube and we received 1,000 cc's of glucose. Almost immediately I could feel the strength begin to come back into my body. I forgot what it felt like to be functionally healthy. My memory of it came back as soon as I felt the life energy begin to serge back through my muscles. It took less than five minutes for that glucose to start taking effect. It also left the taste of peanuts in my mouth. After feeling some of my strength come back into my body, which was not much, I was beginning to realize how far gone I actually was. Just from the little bit of help I had received I was already beginning to feel a thousand percent better, and I still had a long way to go. Then again, remembering back to the last hour on the raft, I knew I was going to die that night, which was this night. It all made sense. I was so depleted of my life force that any assistance I received that supported my life was going to make it seem like I made major gains. I had slipped right to the doorstep of death, and just as I was ready to knock on the door God intervened. It was not my time to go, so God stepped in, and that was just fine with me. I now knew that I slipped about as far as one could slip and still be able to return. I thought about what the pilot said. He said if we had been ten minutes later he would have had to put off the rescue until morning. That delay would have certainly taken me past the point of no return. In fact, I honestly feel that I was within an hour and a half from the point of no return. I truthfully felt that when the sun set that evening so too would have my life. Sincerely, that would have been the last sunset I would have ever seen. But here I was, rescued and being nursed back to life.

Bob Hicks, Freeman Hetzer and Elmer Renner all fell asleep almost immediately. However, I on the other hand wanted to celebrate. I asked if there was a chaplain on board. The medic said, "He's already on his way down to see you guys." When he arrived I was so pumped up about the miracle of our rescue that I had to tell him everything. He did not get a chance to ask questions. As soon as he stepped in, my mouth started running. There I was trying to tell him how to preach and tell other sailors how to get their prayers answered. I told him of our prayers of faith and the celebration in the forty-five minutes prior to being spotted by the Corsairs. After about an hour of continuous talking and excitement, the chaplain yelled to the medic to come over and give me a shot so we could all get some sleep. That was the only thing that was going to shut me up that night, and it did.

Before they injected me with sleeping juice, the chaplain explained to me that I should write a letter home as soon as possible, because things were in somewhat of disarray due to the end of the war, and that the Western Union telegram may take quite a while before it reaches my wife and family. After that, they put me to sleep because I was having trouble doing it voluntarily.

The next morning we were told that each of us had lost about 29 pounds in the six days of our ordeal. I went from 148 pounds to 119. I could not believe my weight. I was not very big to begin with being 5'10" and there was almost no fat on me either. But apparently it was mostly water weight and some of the muscle protein. I knew that by being rescued and in the hospital I would re-hydrate and be able to rebuild my muscle with the right foods. The most important thing is that I was off the raft and in a position to begin healing myself.

When I found some time the morning after our rescue, with shaky hands, I wrote my wife a one-page letter telling her that I was rescued and doing just fine, and that I would be home soon. Trying to write that letter was tough. Not just because of my shaky hands, but also because my head was still fairly cloudy and straight thinking was a difficult task at that time, but it was getting easier. I sealed it up, and sent it off.

I was starving and wanted to eat everything in sight, but the four of us were not allowed to eat freely. Instead, we were all given a half a piece of toast and half a cup of coffee for our very first breakfast after our rescue. It felt like torture, but we were getting more in our bodies with our first breakfast than we received while out on the raft for the entire six days. They also said that eating the way we wanted to would only make us sick and do more harm than good. The way they were feeding us was allowing our bodies to slowly come back into a healthy functioning balance. That way, things would go back to normal without the interference of becoming even sicker before we grew better.

Every day they would give us just a little bit more than the previous day. In fact, they would double about what they gave us on the previous day. They would give us our toast and coffee for breakfast, a little bit of soup with some crackers for lunch and a very small portion of mashed potatoes for dinner. It took about six days before we were allowed to eat and drink all that we wanted. When they finally let us eat freely I think I stuffed more food in my body that first day than all the weight I lost through the six days on the raft. I also had this incredible desire to stuff myself with countless Snickers bars. I would eat one and it would taste so good that I would have to eat another and another and another. I just kept eating them and I loved it. It was a beautiful experience.

It was also after our sixth day on the Pine that we were ordered to go to a Marine Tent hospital on the island of Okinawa. We were also told that three of us would go to Okinawa and one of our buddies, Elmer Renner, was being sent down to Guam for further treatment. They did not tell us exactly why, but they hinted that it was because he was in worse shape than the rest of us and needed a little extra TLC.

We climbed off of the ship and they carried us over to the island in a small boat. The medical personnel in the tent were very kind and caring. When they found out what we had gone through they were very congratulatory, compassionate, gentle and thoughtful toward us. They kept the all we could eat meals coming and they continued to satisfy my craving for Snickers bars. One time while I was eating with Hicks and Hetzer, I looked over at Hicks and said, "Bob, after you offered us your body on that sixth day, you were beginning to look pretty good to me. I was so hungry, I almost started to take bites out of you while you were still alive." Of course I was just joking and the three of us had a good laugh.

We had been cared for and pampered for five days in this tent when an officer approached us with some interesting information. He told us that two other men from our ship had been rescued. The first one, George Wade, was pulled out of the water the morning after our ship went down. He never made it to the raft, but apparently he was able to escape the sinking ship and survive the typhoon with just his life jacket. He was picked up about 5:00 p.m. on September 17. It was a horrible experience among the safety of the life raft and I could only imagine that it must have been a thousand times worse with just a life vest. The three of us were very happy to hear that George Wade made it through the ordeal.

The second one was the boy that I gave my life jacket to, Wayne Neyland. After we watched him swim off out of sight, a Japanese patrol boat picked him up. I concluded since he did not tell them about us because when they pulled him on board, he was too weak to tell anybody on the ship that there were still seven of us out there on a raft floating aimlessly. I figured he basically collapsed from exhaustion. However, there was something about this idea that bothered me. I could not pin point it at this time so I quit thinking about it. I just thought that it was awfully strange that Wayne was able to swim and get picked up, but he was unable to tell anybody that there were still seven of us out there. Something just did not seem right to me. Wayne was the youngest man on the ship and he was a very confident and sometimes self-absorbed individual. At this time I wondered if his self-absorption was actually pure selfishness being content with his own rescue when he was finally picked up. I did not want to think too much about it because I had too many good things to focus on at this time, so I let it go for the time being and went about my business.

We found out that there were a total of six survivors from YMS – 472, Freeman, Bob, Elmer, George, Wayne and myself. Two bodies were pulled out of the water the next morning. That was "Doc" Eaves and his pal Jim Hobart. When they were found, their life jackets were tied together. Eaves and Hobart were inseparable shipmates that hit it off immediately. Whenever you saw one of them you knew the other was somewhere very close. They were the best of friends in life and they left this world the same way, the best of friends. I was deeply saddened when the news of their deaths reached me. I said a prayer and thanked God for giving me the time with them that I had.

Out of thirty-one men on board, two were found dead, six were found alive and twenty-three were never seen again. I felt absolutely horrible for all the family members of my twenty-five comrades who would not be going home alive. It was ironic how all thirty-one of us had survived the mine sweeping adventures in the Atlantic Ocean with out a scratch. We experienced the end of the war in Europe – made it through the Panama Canal, across the Pacific, then heard of the Japanese surrendering unconditionally. We survived attacks from enemy submarines, an assortment of mines and any form of military conflict only to be stopped by Mother Nature's fury. The enemy never gave us any real problems. It was the weather that inevitably destroyed our ship and took the lives of my shipmates. It was a tough concept to digest because I could not swallow it. It just did not seem fair. Several of them had children, and the thought of these children not seeing their daddies again just ripped my heart out. I was actually beginning to feel some guilt about the whole situation. It just did not seem fair that I was still here and going home, but they were never seen or heard from again. I did not like this concept.

George Wade who was picked up out of the water the next day eventually said that when the ship went down there were thirteen sailors from the ship floating in the storm holding hands and forming a circle. He said that "Doc" Eaves and "Doc's" best friend Jim Hobart were in that circle. However, the shifting brine was too powerful and the thirteen sailors were eventually separated. Apparently, Eaves and Hobart decided to tie their life jackets together at this point. That meant that twenty-two men were known to make it out of the ship and nine others were unaccounted for. That does not necessarily mean they went down with the ship. It just meant that nobody knew if they made it out and succumbed to the elements, or actually did go down with the ship.

The news of my shipmates was horrible news to say the least. Even though I was alive and I knew I was going to see my family again, I was devastated over the fate of my comrades. At this point I could not let myself dwell on it, so I decided to pay attention to the points of light in my life. I had my family to look after. I also knew that God was in control and I was still alive for a reason. So, in order to keep me from slipping into a depression, I thanked God for the rescue and promised that every good deed I did from this point on would be to honor God as well as my shipmates. I still had my whole life ahead of me and the least I could do was honor my military brothers through doing God's work. I made a promise to God that if I were rescued I would do all within my power to further God's cause and I was going to keep that promise with one added stipulation. I would attach my shipmates to that promise and honor them, as they so rightly deserved it. It was the least I could do for such a fine group of men.

Recovery was slow but certain in the hospital. Every day I was feeling stronger and healthier. After about a week, when we were allowed to eat and drink all we wanted, some very good news reached our ears. We were happy to hear the officer from our fleet headquarters say that we three would be flying home, and because of our experience we would not be reassigned. He said as soon as we recovered we would ferry out to his ship, we would journey to Hawaii, and we would be given written orders to fly home from there. It almost did not seem true. I sometimes felt like I was dreaming. To think that just a few days before I was within a few hours of my death on a military raft. Now, all of a sudden, I was going to be discharged from the service and flown home to be with my family for good. I really could not see how life could get any better than that. I was euphoric, and extremely thankful. There was nothing more I could ask for. I had everything I could ever need at this point.

We spent fifteen days on Okinawa in the tent recovering and healing. It was exactly three weeks to the day that our ship went down when we were given our orders to head home. We were not given much time, so we gathered what little belongings we picked up on the island and with excitement, we were headed out to a ship to get orders to fly home. On the way out there the boat operator said that the ship we were to get our orders from had gone over to get fuel. He then told us that his orders were to drop us off on the L.S.T. that was anchored right next to the spot where our ship would be anchored. When our ship came in we were supposed to be transferred and begin our journey home. We climbed aboard the L.S.T. We walked to our waiting spot and we had hardly set our bags down when we heard the anchor chains winding in and the engines cut in. We were not exactly sure what was going on. We wondered if they were actually taking us to the ship that would be taking us to Hawaii. Curious, I stopped a sailor running by and asked him what was going on. He said, "We just got the message that another typhoon was headed our way." The word "Typhoon" echoed in my head like a recurring nightmare. I thought I was hearing things. However, the sailor's actions were so hurried that I knew it was for real. At this point Bob Hicks, Freeman Hetzer and I became three severe basket cases. We went into a high gear panic. Crying and screaming, we ran to the bridge and began to try to convince the captain to lower a lifeboat over the side and we would do our own paddling to shore. We explained our ship sinking three weeks prior to this day and we explained our whole raft experience. The skipper replied, "240 men aboard this ship are depending on me. I cannot spare a second." I then asked the skipper if he could just go as close to the tip of the island as possible, and we would jump in and swim to shore. His final words to me were, "Hang on, I'll get you out and back safely." We were not very comforted by those words. I had never been more stressed out and worried at any other point in my life. It felt like monkeys were jumping up and down in my stomach and eating it one small piece at a time. I thought I might die before the typhoon ever reached us. This could not be happening again, I thought.

The three of us immediately put on life jackets, then went down to the galley and started wiring small cans of food, water and supplies to the life jackets. We began to look a little different from all the rest of the sailors on board. We were the only sailors onboard that looked like walking supermarkets. The other sailors were very good to us. After hearing about our experience, we had sailors lined up to give us supplies. They felt compassionate toward our neurotic states of mind.

After we were supplied with enough goods to last a month, we went topside. We did not know it at the time, but the typhoon we were about to enter was more severe than the one that sank our ship. It was the most intensely frightening event of my life being on that flat bottom L.S.T. riding a more intense typhoon than the one that sank the Y.M.S. – 472. The wind and the waves gradually picked up and we started going up and down on the swells. They just seemed to keep growing in size. I kept waiting for their size to peak, but it seemed to take forever. Up and down we went, again. The waves just kept growing in height and we would rise up the front, fall off the back and slap the trough between the giant waves. It was frighteningly reminiscent of the YMS – 472 experience. In terror I did the only thing I could do. I held on, waited and prayed.

As I stood there helpless I could see shuttering ripple down the hull, as large waves began to crash into the bow. It looked a lot like a flat piece of foam rippling with the waves in a swimming pool after someone dives in. I could not believe it was actually happening again. I continued to stand there helpless as I watched the ship begin to collapse before my very eyes. The guide wire insulators began to break and a large portion of the mast and radio tower came crashing down on deck. I had a hard time accepting what I was seeing. I could not believe it was happening again! I thought by surviving the first typhoon we were home free, but here we were again. Being the anxiety riddled, nervous wreck that I was, I imagined that this is what the middle of hell must feel like. To make matters worse I heard the message we all dreaded hearing over the loudspeaker, "All men not on duty put life jackets on and prepare to abandon ship." I felt like I was caught in a bad dream that I could not wake up from. This could not be happening again. To say the word unbelievable was an understatement. I was completely beside myself and dismayed at my misfortune. It was actually going to happen again, I thought. I would fall victim to two typhoons in one month and I just wanted to die on the spot. What are the odds? The thought of floating on the Pacific Ocean in a naval raft again was sickening to say the least. I honestly did not know if I could handle another experience like that. I thought my heart would give out before we were forced to abandon ship. Once again, here I was having thoughts of wanting to be home with my relatives. I was missing Ida and my son Richard. I wanted so bad to be at a family gathering at this moment with all of my kin. But these thoughts were short-lived and unreal. I had to force myself to concentrate on the moment. I was caught in a huge typhoon and it was not going away anytime soon.

The only thing I was able to do to alleviate some of the tension was pray. God pulled me through the first time, and I knew God would do it again. With my eyes wide open and hanging on tight, I prayed silently to myself. At this point, my thoughts were, 'God did not save me from one typhoon to kill me in a second typhoon.' With this reminder of my faith coming through the first time, I noticed some of the tension beginning to leave me. At the beginning of this typhoon I was flooded with the most intense stress I had ever felt in my life, but it was beginning to lift somewhat. I was actually able to relax a little, very little, during the many hours of anguish. My lesson in faith kicked in and I actually was able to finally accept the circumstances without fear. However, the anguish and stress were abundant. Once again, I thanked God for the answer before it came. Before the typhoon was over I thanked God for letting me be okay.

Within an hour of hearing the "Prepare to abandon ship" message, we heard a second message over the loud speaker. It said, "We have orders to turn back and be on the look out for survivors from sunken ships." So, for the next several hours we patrolled the chaotic waters attempting to spy survivors while struggling to survive ourselves. The LST was larger than the YMS – 472 and seemed to take on the typhoon with a little more security, but it was not enough to relieve all our suffering.

It was about twelve hours of pure torment for the three of us. In the typhoon that sank our ship there were a total of nine ships lost. We found out later that there were a total of twenty-nine ships sunk in this typhoon. In our search for survivors we drew closer to Okinawa. The skipper sent an officer to our location on the ship. He said to us that the captain wanted us to go to the launch area and go in for a transfer to receive written orders to fly home. We had to wait for the water to calm down enough so we could safely cross it and it felt like it would never happen, but we were finally being lowered over the side of the ship at the same time the anchors were being lowered. The unbelievably, hellish nightmare was finally over, we hoped. The small boat we were being lowered in hit the water before the anchors did and the three of us were the happiest sailors the world could have ever experienced at the time.

We made our way to our flagship where we would pick up orders to fly home. It was across the bay about 500 yards. When we arrived we walked up the gangway and into the operations office. I was suddenly surprised to see one of my hometown buddies, Lee Parish, who was stationed on this ship. He was a dear friend from back home in Orange, Texas. As we entered the waiting room, I was again surprised to see the skipper of our sister ship the YMS – 454. I asked him if he was there to receive orders to go home. He answered no, and went on to say that he was there for a hearing on the beaching of his ship. He told me that on the night our ship went down in the typhoon his ship's crewmembers could hear our distress cries for help, and after he had learned of only six men surviving out of thirty-one the entire crew voted to beach the YMS – 454, in the second typhoon, in order to avoid a similar situation. They ran their ship up on the beach in the very early stages of the typhoon in order to avoid any possible deaths from sinking. They played cards on the sand, and not a single man was lost. However, the

Navy was not happy about that and the skipper had to wait and see what his fate would be. Apparently, the surge was up when he beached it. After the typhoon passed and the water level went back to neutral the YMS – 454 was several hundred feet up the beach. I never heard how they put her back in the ocean or even if they were able to, but in any case the skipper was in the hot seat. I remember he told me that when they were close to the beach he told the helmsman to gun it. They ended up riding in with the waves like a surfboard and stopped right on the beach. I wished him the best, told him to keep the faith, said God bless and shook his hand. That would be the last time I ever saw him and I never heard what actually happened to him.

When we finally received our orders to fly home, we were taken to the U.S. Army Air strip on Okinawa Island. When we arrived we stepped out and began walking up the path to the airstrip. We were shocked by all the destruction the typhoon had dealt to the area. The place was devastated. It looked like a war battle came through the area. Off to our left we could see where the roof had been completely blown off of the mess hall. There was so much debris littering the ground that it was very similar looking to a public dump. As I was walking I caught a very faint scent of decaying flesh and looked to my right. Almost immediately I was stopped in my tracks by what I saw. At first I thought my mind was playing tricks on me, but the more I stared the more I realized the ugly scene I was witnessing was actually real. There before me, floating in the bay, were about one hundred dead and bloated sailors who had washed in from the Pacific Ocean. They were killed in the typhoon the three of us had just survived. These sailors were stacked one next to the other, gently bobbing with the rise and fall of the small waves. They were all wearing their Navy blue clothing, and some of them still had on their white hats. The typhoon snuffed out their lives like a fire never to burn again, and yet I could not help but think that there had not been the decency for the military to give them a proper burial. Even though there had not been enough time, my emotions at that moment had no logic. I thought to myself, 'they were just left to float there like refuse in the bay.' Even through my whole experience of watching my buddies die, go crazy and disappear, nothing hit me harder than that moment when I witnessed those poor boys floating like debris in the harbor. I had hardly cried a tear through my six-day tribulation, but in that moment as I was staring, it was as if somebody turned on a faucet and I could not control the tears that began pouring down my cheeks. Maybe I was crying for those boys in the harbor, or maybe they reminded me of my buddies that did not make it home. Either way, the thought of those poor boys just floating in the harbor was haunting and it just made me sick to my stomach. I thought about their parents and what they would think if they knew their sons were floating in this harbor like small pieces of driftwood that go unnoticed. This, by far, was the toughest emotional event I had encountered through my whole war experience. All I could think about was that I hoped somebody would find the time to take those poor boys out of the water and give them the proper burial they so rightly deserved. My heart truly, truly ached for them, and all I could do to relieve some of the pain was to let the tears flow. With my tears flowing, and for unknown reasons to me, I stood there at least five minutes starring at the detestable scene and taking it all in before I finally moved on. I could not believe what I just saw. It was definitely the most grotesque sight I had ever witnessed in all my life.

My walk across the airstrip was a very somber one. I was grateful to be alive, but saddened by what I saw in the harbor. I had to focus on the fact that I would be seeing my wife, son and family members in the near future. That was the only thing that kept my mind off of the gut-wrenching scene I had witnessed. It seemed the further from the harbor I went, the further the sadness went. Eventually, I had to push it out of my mind in order for me to make it through the day without crying.

We learned later that the second typhoon was much more severe than the one that sunk our ship three weeks prior. The winds were estimated to be around 120 miles per hour in the first typhoon. In the second typhoon the winds were estimated to be around 150 miles per hour. Once again, God worked a miracle in my life. After seeing that L.S.T. start to come apart in the violence, there is no way we should have survived that category 4 hurricane after the category 3 sank our minesweeper. It had to be divine intervention, because I do not know of too many people, other than the three of us, who survived two giant typhoons with little or no damage. Especially after the first one nearly killed them. God definitely had a purpose for us.

That afternoon we walked through the chow line for our evening meal. We were still underweight and stuffing our selves like pigs every chance we got. In fact, we stuffed our selves so much that I was literally beginning to notice stretch marks on my stomach. Once they turned us loose on all we could eat I had a constant bulge protruding from my stomach from that day until several weeks after I arrived home.

As we sat down to eat, I looked up. It seemed strange because we were eating dinner in a mess hall with no roof. We may as well have eaten outside, because when we looked up all you could see were stars. The date of this meal happened to be October 10, 1945. I found out years later that my nephew, Ovie Broussard Jr, was working in the mess hall on October 10, 1945. He was the older brother to my nephew Benny Broussard. Benny was the one that I clobbered with the dirt clod when we were kids. It would have been great to see him. He was probably working in the kitchen and we didn't even know each other were there. Unfortunately, he died three months later in a plane crash during a mail run to the Philippine Islands. According to the Philippine natives, the C – 47 he was in was coming in for a landing in some very turbulent weather. It was probably the beginning of another typhoon. As they were on their final approach, one of the wings just broke off and the plane spiraled right into the bay. There were no survivors. It really would have been nice to see him one more time before he passed away.

After dinner we headed in the direction of the airstrip. We noticed a small campfire next to the place we were heading. A young Marine attached to the Army Air Corp. as a security guard invited us to spend the night with him around the fire ring. That sounded like a great idea to the three of us, so we decided to join him. As we sat around the fire with our new companion, we enjoyed the coffee he was making over the fire in a gallon can. We had a great time with simple conversation and good laughs. The three of us were not interested in sleeping at all that night for fear that the plane we were scheduled to take would leave without us in the morning. We really wanted to get home more than anything at this time so we did not sleep at all that night.

At daybreak, after thanking our Marine companion, and without a wink of sleep, we were waiting at the plane when the pilot and crew arrived. We were informed that we would make a stop at Guam and the Johnson Islands before heading for Pearl Harbor. It didn't matter where we stopped. The thought that we were finally heading home made the idea of stopping at different islands seem trivial. I was told that since I was the senior enlisted survivor, I would have to layover one day for ships inquest in Pearl Harbor. That was just fine with me since I knew Pearl Harbor was much closer to home than Okinawa. We finally boarded the plane and off we went. I felt like a kid at Christmas time. I was so excited about getting home that I was practically squirming with anticipation. I almost could not control myself. I was finally off the ships and heading out of typhoon country. For a while there this was something that I did not think would ever happen, but it was really finally happening. The trip took about twenty – four hours, but twenty – four hours of traveling with food and water was nothing compared to six days on a raft with no food or water. This trip was a piece of cake.

We arrived at Pearl Harbor the next morning. I was escorted to a building on Ford Island where I entered a big hearing room. I had never seen so much gold, brass and stripes in my whole life. There were Navy officers, Admirals, Captains and every high ranking military person one could imagine. Mixed in with all this brass were news reporters from the Associated Press. I was asked to give a complete report of the sinking of our ship and a day-by-day account of the six days on the raft without food or water. Little did I know that the Associated Press would dispatch my entire account of the experience throughout the world. As a result, my wife, Ida Mae Campbell Harrison, received a call from a church friend that evening. She was told to turn on her radio to a certain station. There was a newsman broadcasting my survival account of our experience and that I was due to arrive in San Francisco the following day. Needless to say, my wife was quite excited to hear my voice. She knew that I was alive and well, but hearing me actually speak was extremely comforting to her. She could tell that I was in good shape.

Upon departing Pearl Harbor, Bob Hicks, Freeman Hetzer and myself were shipped our separate ways. I was flown to San Francisco, while Bob and Freeman were sent back to California by ship. I felt bad for them, because as far as we were all concerned we had more ship experience than a hundred people would want to know in a hundred lifetimes. They groaned at this news and I apologized to them, but there was nothing any of us could do. We exchanged contact information, said our good-byes, shook hands, gave hugs, wished each other well, then went our separate ways. I knew I would be seeing them again, but right now my mind was focused on getting home.

When my flight landed in San Francisco, there was a very large, black limousine waiting for me on the airstrip. It had the American flag, as well as a few other flags, from front to rear. The Naval officer standing by the Limo informed me of my orders from the 11th Naval District to be escorted down town to the upper floor area to the President's office of P.G.&E., Carl Fisher. P.G. & E was actually Pacific Gas & Electric. It was the power company for the whole bay area. That included San Francisco, Oakland, San Jose and all the other areas in that place. Talk about a country boy being out of his element, I was so excited I forgot to kneel down and kiss the ground of my beloved U.S.A. I had never seen a limo before, much less ridden in one. I was not sure what was going on, but I liked it. I was not being given the golden treatment; I was being given the platinum treatment.

On the way up to the President's office the naval officer briefed me on the President's situation. As we entered his office I was very much aware of his emotional state. He had been notified that his only son, and only child, was missing in the same typhoon that sunk our ship. When I stepped into his office to meet him, he approached me, shook my hand, and then gave me a big hug. When he pulled away from me his eyes welled up and tears began running down his cheeks. He was having a difficult time speaking through all of his tears, but he finally asked me if there was any hope that his son could have survived that typhoon. I told him of our miracle rescue and how God, thru prayer and faith came to our rescue. He asked me if we could see any islands in the area. I said yes and that it is a possibility that he could have ended up on one of the many islands in the area. I went on and told him not to give up and that he should check all the islands in the area before he gave up hope. With tears still streaming down his face, he congratulated me on my return home, then gave me a warm hug and sent me on my way. I had never seen a man weep so much in all my life. The tears were literally pouring down his face. This man's story touched my heart, and even though he did not want this to happen, I did feel some guilt after meeting him. I felt sad for this father who lost his only child. Being the father myself of only one boy at the time, I could really understand his pain. I ached for the man, but I had to push it aside because I had to attend to my own son. He offered me a job at P. G. & E and really tried to get me to stay in the bay area, but I told him that my family was all down in the L.A. area. I honestly think he wanted me in the area to have me around as a son. For reasons unknown to me I am pretty sure he thought that I could replace at least a small part of the hole that his son's death created.

Within two hours of my arrival we were on our way to my final Navy assignment. I was to return all our ship's mail to the senders. As I looked at this returning mail it was difficult to know that these letters would never reach my buddies. In fact, it was a difficult thing to have to deal with. Seeing their names on the envelopes and the family members names on the return mail brought tears to my eyes. Just to know that the ones left behind were not going to see their loved ones again was killing me. Once again, I felt guilty that I was here and they were gone. With every little reminder my guilt seemed to grow a little bit bigger.

My wife Ida was able to come up to San Francisco while I was doing this job. Boy what a joy that was. There are no words in existence that can describe how perfect if felt when I wrapped my arms around my beautiful wife and gave her the biggest hug and kiss I could possibly give. Instead of feeling like I had died and gone to heaven, it was as if heaven had come to me. While I was hugging Ida, I realized that my prayers out on the raft were officially answered. At last, I was home.

Back Home

CHAPTER 7

The four of us were plucked out of the water shortly before dark on September 22, 1945. Four days later, on September 26, 1945, while we were recovering in the hospital on Okinawa Island, the news of my missing finally reached my family. I had no idea they had not heard of my missing or my rescue at this time.

My wife Ida Mae had no reason to think I was in any danger. After all, the war had been over for several months in Europe and Japan had surrendered in mid August. As far as she knew I was sweeping the waters around Okinawa Island in post war clean up activities. She thought I would be coming home as soon as we were done with the clean up, and as far as she was concerned, I would be coming home for good. She was already starting to have thoughts of family and togetherness without the interruption of war. She was already making plans for our first family dinner upon my homecoming. Since the end of the war she was no longer concerned for my safety in view of the fact that there were no more enemies trying to stifle my existence. Everything in her mind was worry free, good and everything in the future looked more than promising. However, everything changed for Ida when the doorbell rang on September 26. When Ida answered the door my sister Floy was standing there with an expression of fear and concern on her face. Floy said, "There is a telegram for you at the telegraph office. It is from the Washington Navy Department." Puzzled and anxious with worry and a little bit of fear, Ida left the house with Floy.

The telegram came to the Western Union Train station in Pico, California. It was the only telegraph office in town. The man in the office did not have Ida's phone number, because Ida was staying with her mother at this time. Instead, they had my mother's phone number, so they called her instead. My mother then called my sister's house and relayed the message that there was a Western Union telegram waiting at the telegraph office for Ida.

Floy drove Ida to their office and walked in with her. As Ida began to open the envelope she read enough on the outside to send fear and heartbreak running through her body. The telegram read:

87

WASHINGTON DC 641pm Sept 26-45
MRS IDA G MAE HARRISON
IDEEPLY REGRET TO INFORM YOU THAT YOUR HUSBAND
HERBERT RALPH HARRISON FIREMAN FIRST CLASS USRN IS
MISSING AS A RESULT OF A TYPHOON ON 16 SEPT 1945 IN THE
SERVICE OF HIS COUNTRY YOUR GREAT ANXIETY IS APPRECIATED
AND YOU WILL BE FURNISHED DETAILS WHEN RECEIVED.
VICE ADMIRAL LEWIS BENFELD THE CHIEF OF NAVAL
PERSONNEL

When Ida Mae read that telegram, my sister Floy said Ida turned pale like a ghost as her face dropped. Ida's first thoughts were, "No! This cannot be true. There must be some kind of mistake." She composed herself well, but her heart skipped a few beats as she hoped it *was* a mistake, or just a bad dream. Floy asked what it was. Ida silently handed Floy the telegram. Floy read it her self. Completely stunned and taken back by the news, they both jumped back into the car and headed to my parents home.

My parents made the move out to Whittier, California in 1944 around the time my son Richard was one year old. Before they made this move, my sister Floy and her husband Bud Thompson were already living in California with their three boys. After mother gave me her message from her answered prayer that people who enlist on the east coast seem to be stationed on the west coast and people enlisting on the west coast seem to be stationed on the east coast, I was heading for the west coast. I made the move out there to stay with my sister, brother-in-law and my nephews in 1942 while I was waiting to be enlisted into the navy. This was also the day when Floy told me that there was a young lady at church she wanted me to meet. The next morning at church is when I met Ida Mae and like I said before, it was hopeless for both of us, and we knew from day one that we were right for each other. It was definitely in God's plans that Ida Mae and I were meant to be together. Our courtship was only a couple of weeks when I proposed to her. I knew she was going to say yes, because it was as if our future was written in the stars. We were both elated because we knew it was not only the right thing to do in God's eyes, but also the only thing to do. I never knew a simple guy like me could ever find true happiness in California. That was one of the last things on my mind, but when it happened I went with it and it was just fine with me. It was wonderful to say the least. Words could not describe how good it felt. This experience gave a whole new meaning to my personal existence. The emotions I experienced were delightful. My life took on a whole new direction and a whole new purpose at this point.

Originally I went out to California to join the Navy immediately. The intention was to go to California, join the Navy and get on with my military experience. But, after meeting Ida Mae, I did not enlist right away like I planned on doing. I wanted to spend as much time with Ida Mae as possible. I prolonged my voluntary enlistment until I received word from my mother back in Orange, Texas that the war department sent a letter there in my name and they were about ready to draft me into the Army. Not wanting to be a grunt in the Army, I immediately enlisted in the Navy. Ida Mae and I were planning on getting married just before I was sent away to basic training. Before I met Ida Mae I was dead set and excited about joining the Navy. After meeting Ida Mae the thought of joining the Navy seemed more like a thorn in my side because I knew it was going to take me away from her for extended periods of time. I still wanted to join, but what I really wanted to do was spend everyday with Ida Mae.

When my mother and father received word that I was engaged, they rode the train out to California in the summer of 1942 to meet Ida Mae. They had to meet this young lady I was so enthralled with and when they did they absolutely loved her. Up until that point my parents had never been outside of Texas. Unexpectedly, while they were in California, they realized they liked it. They loved the fair weather. They loved the different life style, and they loved the fact that there were far more opportunities for them to have a much more comfortable lifestyle than there were in Orange, Texas. My mom and dad basically fell in love with the place and they made definite plans to move there someday.

Never being out of Texas up until this trip opened them up to a whole new reality. Both my parents were born in Center, Texas, my father Jack Harrison was born on March 26, 1882 and my mother Zella Holt was born on September 17, 1887. My father's parents, Ely Harrison and Elizabeth Harrison, were farmers in Center, Texas. They farmed cotton for clothing and sugar cane for syrup. The farm right next door to theirs belonged to John Wesley Holt and Mary Tabitha Holt. They just happened to be my mother's parents. My mom and dad were neighbors growing up and by growing up together they became quite fond of each other. Unfortunately, at this point in history it was common practice for the parents to promise their daughter or daughters to someone's hand in marriage. The women did not have any say in who they would marry. My grand parents had promised my mother's hand in marriage to a very wealthy man whose name mother never shared with us. Mother knew that marrying the man my grandparents picked out for her was not the right thing to do even though tradition said it was. Mother always followed her intuition over any tradition. This planned wedding was supposed to be a big deal. All the invitations had been sent out and a rather large number of people were invited. Some of the invite's were supposed to be to some very important and wealthy people. Mother never felt right about the whole situation. The idea of marrying a man she hardly knew never made sense to her no matter how much money he had. She absolutely did not feel good about it. Since her parents were basically poor, they were excited about the prospect of their daughter having a life of more luxury than themselves. However, internal happiness was far more important to my mother than outward success, because the night before the wedding my mother went into her closet, closed the door behind her and prayed to God. She said that God revealed to her that her long time interest, neighbor and friend, Jack Harrison, my father, was a good man and would love her, provide for her and meet all her needs under any circumstances. With the carriages already showing up filled with wedding guests, the night before the wedding, my mother snuck out of her bedroom window, ran off with Jack Harrison and eloped at the age of eighteen. Needless to say, my grandparents were extremely disappointed and very embarrassed with my mother's decision. They did not speak to her for at least two years after that incident. However, after enough time passed and my parents first child was born, my grandparents forgave and forgot. They were just happy that their daughter was happy, and they loved their new grandchild.

After my parents were married they gave birth to eleven children with all eleven being born in Orange, Texas. The first to be born was my sister Cassie. She was born August 22, 1905. The second sibling to be born was another sister my parents named Jimmie. This confused people because of the name. Most people thought Jimmie was a boy until her hair grew out. She was born November 9, 1906. The third member of the family was my brother "BJ" which was short for Benjamin Jackson Jr. Unfortunately, BJ passed away at the age of five due to typhoid fever. Typhoid fever is an illness caused by the bacterium Salmonella typhi. It is very common world wide even to this day, and it is transmitted by food or water contaminated with feces from an infected person. Today they have antibiotics that can fight it. Back when my brother passed away, those antibiotics had not yet been discovered. BJ was born and passed away long before I was born, so I never had the chance to meet him. I only knew about him through the stories from my parents and older siblings. The next child to be born was Ima Fay. She was born June 6, 1913. Two years after Ima Fay, my sister Floy was born on September 28, 1915. After Floy was born, my mother gave birth to Floyce. Unfortunately, at the age of two, my sister Cassie was playing with Floyce in a wagon we had. It was a large wagon. It was the type that the pioneers used to cross the Great Plains. Floyce fell out of it and hit her head on the ground hard enough that two months later she succumb to the wounds. She was taken to the doctor, but back then there was no way of seeing the internal damage she had sustained. Mother knew something was wrong, but she did not know exactly what. She passed away at the age of two and I never had the opportunity to meet her either. Years later, my sister Floy told me that one day after Floyce passed mother was out in the front yard broken hearted and crying her eyes out. My brother BJ, who just turned five at the time, went up to mother and said, "Mama, when I get to heaven I think I'm going to give baby Floyce a drink of water right out of the little dipper." Ironically, less than a year later, BJ passed away due to the typhoid fever. I like to think God does work in mysterious ways, and BJ was sent there to keep Floyce company. The next sibling in the line of births was my brother Johnny Royce. We all called him "Red" because of his red hair. He was born November 13, 1917. After Red was born my brother Luther Rae was born. His nickname was "Luke." He was born on November 9, 1919. Red and Luke were the two older brothers I grew up with. That would mean that the next addition to the family was myself. I was born Herbert Ralph Harrison on December 12, 1921. The name Bill was the name everyone recognized me by and I inherited that name from my mom's sister, Aunt Rosie. My aunt asked my mom why she named me Herbert Ralph. My mom's answer was that she read a good book with two very virtuous and good characters in the story. One of them was named Herbert and the other one was named Ralph. My Aunt Rosie said to my mom, "That's a horrible name. His name is going to be Bill." So, Bill it was. In fact, I did not know my legal name was Herbert Ralph until I went to sign up for the Navy. My mother mailed my birth certificate to me and that was the first time I ever saw my real name. I thought my name was Bill. Everybody called me Bill and they printed Bill Harrison on my high school diploma. As far as I knew, my name was Bill. It was actually a little exciting to find out I had a different name than what I thought it was.

The next sibling to be born was my baby sister Helen. She was born May 3, 1925. And, finally, the baby of the family was my baby brother Claude. He was born August 7, 1927. Both Helen and Claude were known as Helen and Claude. My aunt Rosie was just fine with their names.

My parents never had much in terms of money, but they were wealthy when it came to loving their family. There was nothing more important to both my parents than their relationship with God, their Christian heritage and the love for their family. Having so many children during the great depression made it virtually impossible to own any of the luxury items some other families might have had, but somehow my family was always able to receive the basic necessities. We always had food when we grew hungry and we always had a roof over our heads.

Mother was the spiritual cornerstone of our family. Every night she would get the whole family together and read scripture to us. We would all kneel down and listen to her reading before we went to bed. Every morning mother would have us all kneel down again and we would pray before we left for school. Mother seemed to have a direct pipeline to God. Every legitimate request she would ask of God was always answered. I sometimes felt like she was a wingless angel that had been placed here on earth to do earthly work for those who might have needed some spiritual guidance. During the great depression food was a scarce commodity in my family due to the fact that we had no money. After the family would eat the last meal and there was no more food in the house, mother would go into her prayer closet, which was actually a closet, and pray to God. She would say, "You know our predicament and we know you're in charge and we know you'll give us food." She would then thank God for answering her prayer and step out of the closet. Every time we were in this situation and every time mother would pray to God for food, it never failed. Either a neighbor would bring a large pot of stew by the very next morning or we would look out on the porch the next day and there would be food sitting on our porch. Bags of flour would be left on our porch, fruits, vegetables and an assortment of other nourishing morsels. Most of the time we had no idea who would leave them there, but it was there for us to eat and we thanked God for the answered prayers. And like I said, it never failed. Mom's prayers were always answered. God was good to our family.

My sister and my wife finally made it to my parent's house. They entered the home visibly shaken and obviously worried about something according to my mother. They handed the telegram to my mother. She read it and was very concerned when she handed it to my father. My father read it. Stoical was his demeanor when he was finished. He showed no outward signs of distress or worry, but he later admitted to being much more concerned than he appeared. He had no desire to lose any more of his children before it was his time to go. Losing two was hard enough on him and he was in no way ready to have a third one taken from him. My father firmly believed that a parent should not have to see their children go before them. He hoped it was just a mistake, but a deeper part of him knew it was very real and he went back and forth between fearing the worst and knowing I was okay. Even though he showed no outward signs of it, my father was very much on an emotional rollercoaster.

When the words "Herbert Ralph Harrison" and "missing" registered, they were not sure what to think. Was it a mistake? Was it real? Was it wrong? Was it right? It took a little bit of time to sink in, but their uncertainty eventually turned to concern and worry. Like myself, they were wondering how this could be. After all the war was over and there were no more enemies. A sailor like me should only come up missing in time of war, not in time of peace. However, I was officially missing as a result of the typhoon and my family members were not sure what to do about it.

It did not take long for word to spread to all my family members. By this time everybody was living in Whittier, California just a few blocks apart. There were no longer any family members living in Orange, Texas. Once mother and father fell in love with California in 1942, they moved there in 1944. My sisters Ima Fay and Floy were already living there. Johnny Royce, "Red" and Luther Rae, "Luke," were both in the Navy. My younger siblings, Helen and Claude, were still living at home with my mother and my father. The only family members that had to pack up and move out there with my parents were my oldest sisters Cassie Ovie and Jimmie Lee. Cassie and her husband packed up their six children, Jimmie Lee and her husband packed up their two children and they all headed out to Whittier, California with my mother and my father. We were all together like one big happy family until word of me missing found its way to my family. That was when the family went from happy to very concerned and worried. All they could do was wait for another telegram and hope it was good news. I felt bad that they had to go through this torment on my account. The sad thing is that they actually had to go through it after the ordeal was over. That just does not seem fair.

Initially my mother was a little worried. But, eventually she took more of a staunch knowing that I was going to be just fine. She focused her attention on her very accurate intuition that she claimed was a tool God used to communicate with her. Mother said her intuition was the liaison between the physical world and the spiritual world. She had no gut feeling that I was dead or going to die. From this point on my mother stayed strong, faithful and never wavered. She was already beginning to thank God for my rescue and knew it was only a matter of time before it actually happened. Her direct pipeline to God was definitely one of a kind. Because of her history with answered prayers the whole family tended to pay attention to what my mother said. Fortunately her track record had a calming affect on the family members. There were still some deep seeded concerns and a mild doubt now and then, but for the most part it relieved the larger portion of the distress that the family would have experienced otherwise. Without knowing I was recovering in the hospital already, mother had a gut feeling that I was just fine. How right she was. The only problem was that not everybody in my family had my mother's intuition. If they had, I do not think anybody would have worried about anything at all.

My older brothers "Red" and "Luke" were both in the Navy during the war and they knew how powerful a typhoon actually was. They never said anything out loud to any of the other family members, but they did not think my chances of survival were very good. In fact, they pretty much wrote me off as dead. Being the Navy trained sailors they were, a typhoon was something they did not think any human could possibly survive once the ship goes down. Their logic was simple. If the ship cannot survive the typhoon, what makes anybody think a human body could handle it? But, because of my mother's faith, both of them held out for some hope they later labeled as, "Hoping for a miracle." They too knew of my mother's track record. They had their own thoughts, but they never doubted mother's gut feeling. Beyond their own beliefs, mother's words did provide them with some certain comfort.

Ida Mae new that my mother's prayers were going up to God everyday, so she tried not to be too concerned about my safety. Mother's direct link to God had consistently proven itself over and over so many times that Ida did not worry at first. However, it took several hours for all of this to sink into a true realization of what was really happening. At this point Ida Mae kept going back and forth between her faith in my mother's prayers and her own worry.

Ida's first night with the knowledge that I was missing was sleepless. Ida lie awake all night engrossed with an ugly feeling of emptiness eating away at her stomach. Tossing and turning she battled back and forth between her faith in mother's prayers and the revolting reality that was placed upon her earlier in the day. Even with all her confidence in God and real life evidence of many answered prayers, there was still that little part of her that feared the worst. This was a battle that only she knew about. Nobody else could feel it, see it, experience it, or understand it except she and God. At times she felt like breaking down in tears and just bawling. That was mixed in with moments where she knew everything was going to be just fine. She was definitely caught in a severe battle between her faith and her doubt. At times she knew I was going to be just fine, then she would suddenly think that our son Richard was going to grow up without a father. With that thought, her stomach would knot up and she would curl up on her side and bring her knees to her chest. My poor wife was being tormented. Little did she know that I was actually sitting in the hospital on Okinawa Island recovering, and little did I know that my whole family was going through this torment four days after my rescue. Communication was slow in those days. Needless to say, had I been able to, I would have informed them of my rescue immediately after it happened. However, communication was nothing like it is today. We did not have the convenience of email, cell phones or text messaging. All we had was the mail system, and with the growth of technology, this system later became known as "Snail Mail."

By the next day, five days after my rescue, September 27, word had spread through the church my family attended. The entire congregation reached out to my whole family with such pure empathy that they were taken back by the compassionate acts of kindness. There were offers of food, prayer, love and support in ways my family had never experienced before. Some of my family members thought to themselves that if they lost me through this whole ordeal, they would inherit a huge loving and kind family in return, which was the entire congregation. Like all other Americans at that time the worshippers at our church were excited about the war coming to an end, and when they heard that I was missing at a time of peace they were as perturbed by that concept as my family was.

All our church members called for special prayer time and they all prayed for my safe return. Ida's worry was fading away. With all this faith, she said that she knew I was going to be just fine. In fact, her faith was becoming so strong that her sister Dotty made the remark to my mother that Ida was not showing any sorrow or sadness what so ever. Ida said that Dotty did not realize the faith and assurance that she held in the church's prayers and mother's prayers. Even when the Navy Casualty Department sent life insurance forms home, Ida set them aside and did not bother filling them out or reading them. Her faith was impenetrable. She was in the frame of mind that I had a little boy to raise and God was not going to let our baby boy grow up without his daddy.

My mother continued to pray for my safety and she kept saying that God was telling her that I was not dead. This comforted my family members, because of my mother's track record. Mother's prayers went up everyday and as the days past my family's faith grew in strength. Although there was still a fair share of worry, the comfort in faith was beginning to win out. Slowly, but surely my entire family was beginning to feel their faith override the worry that had gripped them for so long. It was a slow process, but it was definite.

About the 30th of September 1945, Ida received another letter from the Naval Department's Bureau of Naval Personnel. This letter was written on September 28, which was six days after our rescue.

Dear Mrs. Harrison:

It is with regret that this Bureau confirms the report that your husband, Herbert Ralph Harrison, Motor Machinist's Mate second class, United States Naval Reserve, is being carried on the official records in the status of missing.

Details in connection with your husband's disappearance have not been received. However, because of the intensive search, which is being carried out in all areas at the present time, information clarifying the status of missing personnel is being received daily. It is hoped that a report will be received concerning your husband in the near future.

Sincere sympathy is extended to you in your anxiety. You are assured that any further information received will be forwarded to you promptly.

You are urged to read the enclosed booklet carefully as it explains matters of importance concerning naval personnel in the missing status.

By direction of Chief of Naval Personnel.

Sincerely yours,
H.B. Atkinson
Commander, USNR.
Officer in charge
Casualty Section

Then, on Monday, October 1, 1945, nine days after my rescue, my mother stepped out of her prayer closet one morning and said to everyone, "I just stepped out of my prayer closet experience with God, and God told me that we will hear from Bill today." Ida said that she knew without a doubt if my mother said it, it was going to happen. All day long Ida waited for the mailman, because she knew there would be some good news about my whereabouts. As time grew closer for the mailman's arrival, Ida was becoming more and more excited. When she finally saw him approach, she ran out to him and dug into his bag before he could hand her the mail. She pulled out the letter that they told me to write the day after my rescue. The letter said:

Dearest Darling & Richie;

Just a few lines to let you (know) I am o.k. in the Hospital ship as you will hear our ship sank in the typhoon along with four others, only four guys off my ship got out alive they were rescued, Hetzer, Hicks Renner and myself. I spent six days on a raft with no food no water – there (were) nine on the raft to begin with but five died later – planes picked us up at sea and now we are all o.k. and I will be home soon – I am o.k.

> *All my love*
> *to you*
> *Bill*

Thank my dear God for answering prayer – my life is his and yours.

Ida read the letter outside next to the mailbox. When she completed it she went running into the house and made the announcement that the letter made it to the house. After it was read out loud to my family members, the worry vanished and the thanks to God began. There were hugs everywhere and huge amounts of relief. My family could not put in words the joy and relief they experienced after receiving that letter. Everybody was hugging everybody else and my brothers were actually somewhat surprised to know that I really did survive this catastrophic typhoon. Whatever chances they gave me were slim, but that day they learned the valuable lesson that God *is* in control, and that true faith always wins out.

Three days after my mother's announcement, on October 4, 1945, another Western Union telegram reached Ida. It read:

I AM PLEASED TO INFORM YOU THAT YOUR HUSBAND HERBERT RALPH HARRISON MOTOR MACHINISTS MATE SECOND CLASS USSNR PREVIOUSLY REPORTED MISSING AS RESULT OF TYPHOON 16 SEPTEMBER 1945 WHILE IN THE SERVICE OF HIS COUNTRY IS NOW REPORTED TO BE A SURVIVOR. UNDOUBTEDLY HE WILL COMMUNICATE WITH YOU AT AN EARLY DATE CONCERNING HIS WELFARE AND WHEREABOUTS. THE ANXIETY CAUSED YOU BY THE PREVIIOUS MESSAGE IS DEEPLY REGRETTED.
VICE ADMIRAL LOUIS DENFELD THE CHIEF OF NAVAL PERSONNEL.

This particular telegram arrived nearly two weeks after we were rescued. The military mail was most definitely moving at a snails pace at this time. I like to blame it on the chaos created from the war ending and thousands of military personnel going home. I would sure hate to think it was irresponsibility, because if it was that would be an absolute crime to have to put family members through that type of torment. It is just a good thing that my letter reached my family right when it was supposed to.

The experience was not turning out to be an incredible lesson in faith just for Hicks, Hetzer, Renner and myself. It also turned out to be an incredible lesson for all my family members and our entire congregation. We got to see first hand what faith and prayer can actually do. A miracle is overcoming the impossible and that is exactly what happened to the four of us. Through truly understanding faith we overcame impossible odds. There really was no logical, reasonable or practical explanation for us surviving that ordeal. We should have died out there like my shipmates, but we were still here and nearly home. In God's eyes, obviously our job was not finished on this earth. We still had a lot of work to do and we were more than happy to get ourselves started.

Word spread fast of my rescue and it did not take long for my church congregation to hear the good news. The next Sunday, Ida and my family went to church to thank God and pray. When they arrived at church the pastors 14-year old daughter walked up to Ida and handed her a piece of paper. On that piece of paper was a poem this young lady took upon herself to write. It read:

God Answers Prayers

I was awfully tired when that telegram came,
that small piece of paper, which bore my name.
With trembling fingers I tore open and read
We regret to inform you he's missing it said.
Not Bill, not my darling, my heart cried in pain.
He's missing it's true, I read it again,
And I sank to my knees by the side of my chair,
And I prayed and asked God, "Please answer my prayer."
Yes I know he's missing the telegram said,
But God gave assurance that Bill was not dead.
I dried my wet eyes and my tears did cease,
For God gave my heart a deep wonderful peace.
Bill's folks were just lovely, the church folks were grand.
But through the darkest hours I knew God held my hand.
And through the worst moments he felt my faith.
He said, "Fear no my daughter your husband is safe."
Then Monday at mail time a letter from him.
I'm safe now my darling I'll soon be home again.
I again fell to my knees by the side of my chair
And thanked the dear lord for answering my prayer.
I then made God a promise that thankful day
I'll love him and serve him until we meet up there.

With all this good news and loving support, Ida finally went back to her initial plan of preparing for our first supper together. She was able to continue on with her thoughts of beginning her own family and their togetherness. She could continue on with the worry free concept that the war was over and there were no more enemies. She could finally continue with the idea that I really would be coming home for good without the interruption of war and the military taking me away from her and Rich. She felt like a roadblock had finally and permanently been removed and she could officially get on with our lives. But this time it was going to be quite a bit more special. A part of her felt like I had returned from the dead and that was just fine with her, as long as I returned alive. Later, my other family members informed me that Ida was walking with a spring in her step and a brighter twinkle in her eye. They also said that her smile seemed to be permanently placed on her face. She was walking around so light that a couple of times they thought she was just going to flap her arms and fly away. According to Ida, everything looked brighter, colors were more intense, flowers smelled better and life was just beautiful.

My brother's were also walking a little lighter. My father was jubilant and talkative when normally he was a very quiet man. My sisters were cheerful to the point of being just a little giddy and they all could not wait until I finally made it home. There seemed to be a permanent sense of delight in the Harrison family. Prior to my experience life was a little average. After my experience, life was quite a bit more appreciated and definitely not taken for granted. My brothers stated that from that point on they were thankful for the very air they breathe, the water they drink, the food they eat, the shelter they lived in and the family they had. God works in mysterious ways and it was nice to know that the good side of my experience was not just happening to me. It was also spilling over into other people's lives as well.

Our congregation was also making plans for a feast and a gathering when I finally made it home. My whole family and circle of friends were elated that I would be returning. They were not just excited for my return, they were also excited about the way God worked his mercy through this entire process, and the gathering was more for praising God than welcoming me home. That was just fine with me. The news of my story and how we were rescued on that last day was spreading through the congregation and the lesson in faith was being told there as well. Some of the people of the church who were not exactly sure what faith was were receiving a lesson on it they would never forget. It was interesting to me that all my life I heard about the word faith and I really thought I knew what it meant, but after my experience I understood what it really meant. This lesson in faith was also happening to members of the congregation. I felt honored to know that God used me for such an incredibly important lesson about faith for so many people who gained so much from it. I did not know it during our six days, but I found out shortly after I arrived home. It turned out to be quite the blessing. That horrible experience on the raft was really having some very positive results in my neck of the woods.

Home Sweet Home

CHAPTER 8

I was finally, and officially, discharged from the United States Navy on the 19th of December, 1945. Three years and two months was my time of duty in the U.S. Navy during W.W. II. After the last month of U.S. Navy service of returning all backed up ship's mail to our ship's crew's families, and receiving my discharge in the San Francisco area, I could hardly wait to get back to Whittier, California to start my civilian life again. To be with my wife and son Richard, and to see my mom and dad as well as the rest of my family members was the only thing on my mind. In fact, it consumed my every thought both in my dreams as well as in my waking life. I would have turned down all the money in the world at that time if it had been in the way of me seeing my family. Even when the President of P. G. & E. offered me a position and said that I would move up in the ranks more quickly than the average person because I think he held a special place in his heart for me being that he lost his son. I was respectfully not interested because the bay area was way too far from my family members. Surviving six days on the raft taught me that there was something much more precious in this world than the material objects so many are in pursuit of. That priceless something was family and loved ones. Objects can be replaced, but moments with loved ones seem to only happen once and never repeat themselves in exactly the same way. I planned on taking all the new memories in with an appreciation that seemed to run much deeper on my way back home than it was when I joined the Navy. I now valued my past experiences with my family ten fold, I was grateful for the present moments with them and I thoroughly looked forward to more future events. Surviving my ordeal seemed to make life much less complicated than I originally thought it was. Events that might have seemed to be mountains were now little molehills. Big deals and problems just did not exist in my world anymore. The fact that I could breath, drink water when thirsty, eat when hungry, enter shelter to exit the elements, be with family and worship the almighty God was the only thing I really needed. Everything else really did not matter. The important substance now embraced me in my life and I was quite aware of it. My reality took on a whole new meaning and I welcomed it with open arms. It was a costly, but priceless education.

The instant I received my discharge papers, I bought a ticket for the next bus out of the Bay area within a matter of minutes. I could hardly wait to get home and I honestly could not wait another second to start my journey out of Frisco. Ida came to see me when I arrived in San Francisco, but she was only able to stay a couple of days. She needed to get back to take care of our baby boy Rich, so I had to ride the bus home all by myself. I was so excited about getting home that the bus did not seem to go fast enough. It was the longest drive of my life, but the most welcomed one. My excitement was so thick I could hardly stand it. Sometimes the exciting butterflies in my stomach felt so big that I thought there was something boiling in my belly.

The bus arrived in Los Angeles on December 20. I could not get off fast enough. Not because it was unpleasant, but because I wanted to get back to home sweet home. I took the Redline the last ten miles toward my home. I looked around the city in which I lived. All the buildings that I was used to seeing were something that I never thought would look so darn good to me. The sidewalks, the buildings, the telephone poles, the trees, the streets and the sound of the traffic were beautiful.

Upon my arrival, my sister Floy and her husband "Bud" were there to pick me up. With big hugs and large smiles we greeted each other. There were even some tears. It was truly a beautiful experience. We jumped into their car and they took me directly to my parent's house. When we pulled up out front it to was absolutely a beautiful sight that I thought I would never see again while out on the raft. We entered the house, and that is where all the tears flowed freely and the hugs were abundant. I was so eager to see everybody that I was not expecting the tears of joy streaming from my eyes. Every one of my family members were there and we could not stop hugging each other. It did not take long for word to get out that I was home, and before I knew it the inside of my parent's house filled up with family, church members and friends. My parent's house was too small to hold everybody so there were people on the porch, front yard and sidewalk. There had to be somewhere between 75 to 100 people present shortly after my arrival. I never had so many hugs in all my life than on that one particular day. The love and support was so thick that I thought I done died and went straight to heaven. It turned out to be quite the welcome home gathering. Of course I must have told the story of our miracle rescue over a hundred times that day, but that did not matter. I was so happy to be alive and home that I would have told it a thousand times more if anybody wanted to hear it.

One of the guests at my parents home was Pastor May. He was the pastor from our church. After he heard my story about my new discovery of true faith, he could not wait for me to get back to church and share that story with the entire congregation. I told him I would do so with pleasure. I had never spoken before such a large group of people in all my life, but I was going to try to do it anyway. I was not sure exactly how I was going to go about it, but Pastor May was really good about helping me out. He gave me a bible and said to use the last three versus of the 91ˢᵗ Psalm.

"14; Because he hath set his love upon me, therefore will I deliver him: I will set him on high, because he hath known my name.
15; He shall call upon me, and I will answer him, and honour him.
16; With long life will I satisfy him, and shew him my salvation."

After I read those passages I could almost not believe how accurate they were. They basically described everything that went on with me before, during and now after my six days of torment. I never stopped loving God. I never stopped calling upon him. I never stopped honoring him during the ordeal, and God definitely "shewed" me with his graceful salvation. I was definitely salvaged. These words sure did make a lot of sense to me now. Before my experience I would have glossed over these words and had no real idea of what they really meant, but now they reached so deep into my soul that I felt like they were written especially for me. Of course I knew that was not true. This verse applies to anybody, anywhere at anytime, but it sure was nice to have such a deep connection with such a simple truth and straightforward bible verse.

The following Sunday Pastor May set up the sermon to where I would talk about my experience. I was so nervous because I had never spoken before a group of people before, and while I was waiting I would look out at all the eyes in the audience and fear would run up my spine. My palms were sweaty, my heart rate was much higher than usual and fear was setting in, but Pastor May was very comforting. He was right by my side and anytime I needed help all I had to do was look at him and he would answer any question I needed or explain something a little easier than I would.

The congregation was full because word was out that I would be speaking about my experience and many people were interested in hearing about it. I told them everything. I spoke about the beginning of the typhoon, how we were capsized, how I was caught underneath a seventy foot wave, I explained each days ordeal and how five men left the raft and four were killed. I told them everything, including my epiphany with true faith. After the sermon I was swamped with curious, happy and grateful people who were truly appreciative of what they learned in terms of the concept of true faith. I felt like a movie star with all this attention and crowd around me. The only thing missing were all the photographers blasting my face with flash bulbs. While all this was going on a particular church member approached me. He was a contractor and he asked me if I would like to go to work in his company. He said he would start me off in clean up for $1.00 an hour and start an apprentice program for me. Of course I accepted. I started going to projects with him immediately. I cleaned up what ever needed to be cleaned up. I worked in clean up for a short while when he asked me if construction was the thing I would like to get involved with. I said yes because the construction part of it looked like something that I would absolutely love to do. After a little research I was lucky enough to be able to buy my first set of carpenter tools for $100 in the G.I. program at no cost to myself. Two weeks after starting as a clean up man, I became a carpenter's helper. At this point my pay was beginning to go up. Within my first year of working I became a journeyman union carpenter. My pay increased and I was always able to find work whenever I needed to. I was always able to meet the rent, pay all the bills and always have food on our table for my family. This was a good thing because it was within three months of my return home that Ida found out she was pregnant with our second child. This was quite a blessing. I could not help but think that just over three months ago I was knocking on death's door, and now I was nine months away from having a second child. Rich was going to have a new sibling. Boy, I was grateful. It was another beautiful experience that I almost thought I would never get to see.

As the days past I began to settle into my new life. By surviving that typhoon I survived an ordeal I probably should not have survived. It was clear to me that God wanted me here for a reason. I also wanted to keep my promise with God, so I got involved in my church and the exchange club. The exchange club was a service club serving our community. In order to make sure that I fulfilled my promise to God for our rescue at sea, I never turned down an opportunity to relate my experience of how, through faith in God, my life was saved in the miracle aboard the raft. Anytime I was asked, I was more than willing to give the talk about our faith filled miracle rescue. I never once turned down an opportunity to share that story with any group of people or any person. There was nothing that was going to keep me from fulfilling my promise to God. When asked, I was honored to share the story with anybody who asked. Eventually word spread about my talk. The Kiwanis Club asked me to speak on several occasions. The first time I spoke at one of their gatherings, I was sent a thank you letter on January 17, 1946. It said:

"Since Tuesday I have had numerous expressions of appreciation for the splendid talk you gave us at Kiwanis. Many of the members felt it was the finest program we have ever had.

Please accept my personal thanks and appreciation for your contribution to the group. We wish for you the very best of everything as you resume life as a civilian."

The Lions Club asked me to speak. After that speech they put a rather long article in their weekly membership letter explaining the details of my experience and how they were reminded of something we all sometimes forget, faith based prayer. I also received a certificate of appreciation from the Lions Club International.

The Bella Vista branch of the Optimist International Club gave me a certificate of appreciation after sharing the story of my ordeal with them. Many different churches asked me to speak. I gave talks at the Church of the Nazarene and the United Presbyterian Church. I spoke at classes in the Calvary Baptist Church. I gave talks at the local Methodist Church in Whittier. I actually gave more than one talk at each of these churches as the years went by. I spoke at the Women's City Club of Los Angeles. I spoke at the American Association of Retired Persons, and the list goes on and on. By the time I gave the last talk of my experience I literally shared my testimony to nearly 1,000 clubs and groups across America. Of course, Coast and Southern Federal Savings and Loan sponsored me. Four percent of their earnings went to spreading the gospel of "Americanism," faith and free enterprise. They categorized me as one of their "Better Speakers." This was such an honor for me to know that I was fulfilling my promise to God and I would never go back on my word. And, as long I am walking this earth, I will never stop fulfilling that promise. Even after leaving this earth I plan on this book continuing to fulfill my promise to God. When I said to God that if he rescued us I would do all within my power to further his word, I really meant what I said.

I worked as a construction worker for five years before I finally became a general contractor. Shortly after earning my contractors license I started a partnership known as Twycross & Harrison Construction. Our partnership remained together for 45 years. In our 45 years, Randy Twycross and I were never inside a courthouse, and we never had to take anyone to court. I knew that during our involvement in construction God was in control, because we were not smart enough to stay out of trouble. Randy and I always tried to use the Golden Rule when with customers and our partnership. Our good fortune was surely under God's directions.

Both of our families had four children. My children were Richard, Lance, Jeanette and Dan. Richard was born June 17, 1943 in Whittier, California. After Richard graduated high school he went to Pasadena Nazarene College for four years. While in college he married Nola, his high school sweetheart. After he graduated he went to seminary at the Nazarene Theological Seminary in Kansas City for three years. Since he was married at the time, he actually worked his way through by working in a cabinet shop. He had one child while attending the Nazarene Theological Seminary, my grandson Mathew Harrison, and when Richard finished I am very happy to say that he was a certified ordained minister. He was invited to serve at the Nazarene church in Whittier as the youth director. He did this for three years until he was hired in Corona, California as the Senior Pastor of the Nazarene church in Corona. Richard had two children Mathew and Jason. Richard divorced and re-married a wonderful lady named Carol; therefore two-step children entered the picture, Michelle and Lisa. Eventually, Richard left the ministry and began a very successful troubled youth recovery program in Clark County, Nevada.

My second child, Lance was born on October 17,1946 in Whittier, California. When Lance was in the fourth grade he entered one of his pieces of art into the school districts art contest and he won an award for his work. This was about the time I was beginning to recognize he had a natural ability for artwork. In high school he was asked to draw the cover for the annual book cover, and he did with pleasure. After high school he attended Rio Honda Junior College in Whittier. After having to give the college instructors tips on how to do artwork he grew tired of the lack of challenge so he discontinued his college effort. He was hired by the telephone company as a sales man in the art department for advertising. Because of his art ability he moved to the top rapidly and for some reason whenever he made it to the top there were no more challenges for him so he would turn to the bottle. Unfortunately, the bottle eventually won out and my son Lance passed away on June 19, 2002 at the age of 55 due to pneumonia and congestive heart failure. A parent should never have to bury their children, but my experience taught me that God is in control. I never wanted to see Lance go, but I was grateful to God that I had 55 wonderful years with my wonderful son. Lance gave us two wonderful grandchildren. Lance Harrison Jr., and Kristen Harrison.

Jeanette, my first and only daughter, was born on February 27, 1950 in Montebello, California. After she graduated high school she went to work for Kelsey Tube Company. They manufactured pipes. She was their secretary for approximately three years when she met her husband Bob. They were married on July 29, 1973 and had four children, Erick Lee Brown, Jeff Brown, Nancy Ruth Brown and Casey Brown. With all these children Jeanette's profession became a stay at home mother while Bob worked for the Union Pacific Railroad. Erick Lee eventually became the parent to Harrison Lee Brown and Austin Brown, two of my great grandchildren. Jeff Brown had Jordan Brown and Elyssa Brown, two more great grandchildren.

My fourth and final child, Dan was born on October 20, 1951 in Whittier, California. While he was in high school I had him working with me in my company on various construction sites. He followed in my footsteps after graduating high school and became a general contractor. He is a general contractor to this day and he has participated in remodeling expensive homes. Prior to this he began his contractors business in retrofitting old buildings up to current earthquake codes. Dan has been married twice. His first marriage he and his wife Mandi could not have children so they adopted Blake Robert Daneil Harrison, who was born on November 1, 1980. At the age of 20, while he was in college, Blake, against every body's wishes purchased a motorcycle. Due to no fault of his own, while he was learning how to ride his new motorcycle in the neighborhood, another young adult who was under the influence ran a red light and hit Blake while he was on his motorcycle. Blake passed away in the hospital 33 days later on September 24, 2001. Dan met his second wife Cheri when she called him in to finish a job the last contractor did not complete. Cheri heard about Dan's good reputation through word of mouth. Cheri had two children, Travis and Jason, therefore I inherited two more grandchildren.

Another miracle in my life, while being on the Coast Federal Savings & Loan Speakers Bureau for six years, was being able to meet all of my speaking assignments while helping to guide our construction company through its many large projects. The majority of our employees were my relatives, which made management much easier. This was important because sometimes I was asked to speak eight or nine times in one week just to relate my Navy experience of being sunk in the typhoon.

Along with the many custom homes and track houses that our company built, we also built 53 churches on the west coast. Twelve were in San Diego, one was in Seattle and the rest were built in Los Angeles. The first church we constructed was the college Avenue Nazarene Church. This was the church I attended so this was very exciting to me. Randy and I came up with a plan that proved very successful. We asked for church member donated labor to hold down the cost, and it worked. Other churches were anxious for us to start construction on their church after seeing our first finished product and the low cost involved. Our fixed profit was 8% of the total cost. We were not greedy. We basically took what we needed, because as far as we were concerned there really was not anything necessary beyond what we needed.

God wanted me here to be part of the church building crew, and I did that with pleasure. After my rescue there was not a single day go by that I would not think of my close and wonderful shipmates that did not survive. I was still here and they were not. So, I decided to myself that every church that I was a part of building I would dedicate it to my fallen comrades. I did not make a big deal of it and I really did not even tell anybody that I was doing this. I just had them in mind while I was building, and for every foundation laid, two-by-four nailed into place and brick cemented into its location, I thought of them and said to myself, and to God, that I am doing this for their kindness, in their memory and in their honor. That was the least that I could do for such a fine group of young men who never made it home.

Six years after the war I had the opportunity to take a trip back to Orange, Texas and visit the place of my birth and childhood. I saw the old farm we use to live on, the school I attended, our old church and the old neighborhood where I would play with "Snow Ball" and Sammy Cooper. Snow Ball and his family were no longer there and I had no idea where they were or how to find them. I am sad to say that I never saw Snow Ball again. Across the street from our old house was the Cooper residence. I went up to the house and knocked. Mrs. Cooper answered the door. It was quite the pleasant surprise to see that the Coopers still lived there and Mrs. Cooper looked wonderful. She let me in and we had a good talk. After a few minutes of conversation I was so excited to see Sammy again that I asked her where I could find him. It was at this point that she gently informed me that Sammy was killed in Normandy on D-Day. I was stunned by this news and to be perfectly honest I was really not ready to hear that. I almost could not believe that my childhood friend whom I would play football, baseball, and hide and seek with was gone. It almost did not seem real. My shipmates dying were one thing, but my childhood friend dying in the war was something I never imagined, considered or expected. I was very shaken by this fact and it actually broke my heart.

I finally left the Cooper's house and I was not sure what to think. With a heavy heart, I eventually left Orange to return home. Many years later I decided I wanted to look into Sammy's death. Upon further research I actually found out that Sammy was not killed in Normandy, France on D-Day. He was in the Army's 134th Infantry Regiment, which was a part of the 35th Infantry Division. They did not land on Omaha Beach in Normandy until July 5, 1944, one month after the big invasion, and they were not committed to battle until July 10th. There first battle was in St. Lo, France. They had at least four days of constant fighting through the hedgerows before they finally took St. Lo. They went from St. Lo to Mortain, Orleans, Nancy, Habkirchen, Germany and the lower Vosges. They were in the Battle of the Bulge in December to relieve the 101st Airbourne Division. They ended up having 10,000 casualties in their 1,500 mile advance. Sammy was killed in action on September 20, 1944. At that point in history the 134th was engaged in a big battle near Nancy, France. If I did my research right it seems that on September 16 the 134th began their assault at the Meurthe River at about five o'clock in the evening. The battle continued for several days and somewhere in all the chaos my childhood friend was killed on the 20ᵗʰ. Apparently they had taken some high ground from the Germans, but the Germans counterattacked. The Americans had to retake it and the Germans counterattacked again. The battle went back and forth for a while, and Sammy was killed somewhere along the way in the seesaw battle. As of this day records show that he has been buried at the Lorraine American Cemetery in St. Avold, France. I have never seen his head stone, but it is comforting for me to know that his final resting place is Plot C, Row 20, Grave 63. I often wonder what would have happened had he joined the Navy. If he did, there was a very good chance he would have survived the war. However, I knew that God was in charge, and everything happens for a reason, but I sure felt for his mother and other family members.

As the years past, I only remained in contact with Elmer Renner. I never saw George Wade again. George was the one who was picked up out of the water the morning after the typhoon. I found out many years later, through Elmer, that George passed away in 1963 just before Christmas. I never found out what the cause was. He would not have been very old at that time. I also learned through Elmer that Bob Hicks passed away in 1990. Unfortunately, I never saw Bob again once we went our separate ways in Pearl Harbor. Wayne Neyland, the one that was picked up by the Japanese patrol boat, according to Elmer, passed away in 1985 due to complications from diabetes. I never saw him again either. The last time I saw him he was bobbing up and down with the swells in the ocean as he swam away with my life vest on, and I was hoping he would be successful and get some help to rescue us. However, help never came from that direction.

I attempted to contact Freeman Hetzer several times shortly after we both made it home. He was living back in Hooversville, Pennsylvania. In my attempts to contact him I found out that he moved somewhere in Ohio almost immediately after he went back to Pennsylvania. I realized I would not be able to find him so I became busy with my own personal life, and gave up trying to contact him. Then, one day in late February of 2005 I received a phone call and it was Elmer Renner. He was letting me know that Freeman Hetzer would be getting a hold of me very soon. Elmer went on to tell me that Freeman's schoolteacher's son, by chance, bought a copy of the book that Elmer wrote. This man knew Freeman from their school days and kept in touch with him. When he read the book he saw the name Freeman Hetzer in it several times so he contacted Freeman and asked him if he was the Freeman the book was talking about. When Freeman heard that Elmer Renner was the author he knew it was talking about him. Freeman then got a hold of

Elmer and Elmer gave him my phone number and address. After getting off the phone with Elmer, it was not more than twenty minutes when the phone rang again and Freeman was on the other end. I was ecstatic. He and his wife were living in Meza, Arizona, which was pretty darn close to my own home in Hemet, California. They had been living there for the last fifteen years. Freeman and his wife decided that they would come out to visit. The last time I spoke with him was in Pearl Harbor when we went our separate ways. When he finally made it out to my house on February 12, 2005, we had not seen, or spoken to each other in 60 years. My son Dan and daughter Jeanette hired a video company to record it and it turned out to be a very nice DVD. It sure was wonderful to see Freeman after so many years. We had lunch and reminisced about our experience. We told each other about how many children and grandchildren we had and we had a wonderful time. Although Freeman was not necessarily a religious man, he had two sons and they both became ordained ministers. He was very, very proud of them.

He and his wife spent the weekend at our home and it surly was a treat. Freeman informed me at that time that he was taking some heart medication due to a bad heart valve. He was scheduled for surgery in the next few months and they were supposed to repair the valve.

After our weekend was up, we promised to keep in touch and said our good-byes, then Freeman and his wife headed back to Meza. About three months later I received word from his wife that Freeman went into open-heart surgery to repair his valve, but the damage was so extensive there was nothing they could do about it. Freeman never made it out of surgery. I was very saddened after hearing this. I thought about our meeting we had after 60 years and I was grateful to God that I had the chance to see my buddy one last time shortly before he made it home to heaven. Freeman was truly a good man and he was the type of person, that no matter what happens, I could never forget him. He and I shared an experience that not many people have the misfortune to share together and even though I did not see him for sixty years, the bond I felt between he and I was just like the bond I felt for my own brothers, and maybe a little stronger.

Elmer Renner and I saw each other quite a bit in comparison to the others. Elmer would spend every February in Phoenix and either I would drive out to see him or he would drive to Whittier to see me. The first time we actually saw each other after we were separated on Okinawa was in 1953. We would see each other off and on over the years. When Elmer would take a business trip out to Southern California, we would visit. But, as we became more involved with our personal lives, family and children, our visiting became less common. After a while our contact with each other was reduced to sending each other cards and letters on the major holidays. Eventually, the contact stopped all together. I did not hear from Elmer until the late eighties when I was retired and living in Hemet, California. Apparently, Elmer's oldest grandson began asking him about his war experience, which prompted Elmer to write an account of his ordeal. When he was finished he sent a copy of it to me in Whittier and just in case I was no longer there, he asked the post office to forward it to my new address. I received it and read all of it. We began to communicate once again. In 1989, after reading Elmer's account of the ordeal, he came out for a visit and we had our first round of golf together. This was the beginning of a short-lived tradition. We probably played a total of five rounds of golf in our retired years over the next decade and we could never agree on whom the better golfer was. I liked to think I was, but Elmer had his moments that put me to shame. Over the years Elmer would hint to me that he had his struggles with the memory of our typhoon and raft experience. His wife Dorothy once told Ida and myself that she would find him down stairs once in a while, in the middle of the night weeping as he relived the horror of the experience. Being able to fully understand his emotions I sure felt for him.

Through the 90's Elmer did some research on the typhoon that sunk the YMS – 472. He was doing this in preparation for his book that he had published in 2004 titled, "Sea of Sharks." Elmer admits in his book that he had one heck of a time living with the memories of that night on September 16, 1945. His book seemed to be a very healthy form of therapy for him. In March of 2000 he sent me a letter with the information his nephew and son-in-law found regarding the typhoon. The name of the typhoon was Makurazaki. Makurazaki is also the name of the city on the island of Kyushu that received the most damage from the typhoon when it came ashore on September 17, 1945. Kyushu is the southern most island on the chain of islands that make up the country of Japan. They reported the wind velocity to be 115 miles per hour when it reached the shore. It was a little bit faster out over the open sea where we were. It destroyed a total of 273,888 homes and the damaged farm land was 128,403 hectare. One hectare is equivalent to 10,000 square meters. That works out to roughly 36 square miles per hectare. There were also 2,473 people confirmed dead and 1,283 people were reported missing. Makurazaki killed a total of 3,756 people in the country of Japan. I found out later that over 2,600 of the dead actually came from the city of Hiroshima. There was so much tree cutting going on there in the mountains around the area for the war effort that when the typhoon hit, mud slides and floods wreaked havoc. Earlier in September a heavy and steady rain began. The rivers were swelling and inching up the banks. When the typhoon hit the already flooded city it finished off what the A – Bomb did not. Bridges that survived the explosion were swept away. Any functional streets were washed out. Foundations were destroyed on buildings that withstood the blast. A team of scientist, from Kyoto Imperial University, who were studying the delayed reactions of the bomb on the people, were nearly all killed along with their patients when the Ono Army Hospital they were in slid down the mountainside and into the sea. To think that six weeks prior, on August 6, the first Atomic Bomb was dropped on them and then they were hit by Mother Nature's fury. Talk about bad luck.

The location of the sinking was known in a general sense, but the location of our rescue was pretty much pinpointed. According to Elmer, we were about forty miles north east from the north tip of Okinawa Island when we sank. We were picked up about eight to ten miles north of Tokuno Jima. According to the map that Elmer gave me, we drifted approximately 70 miles. I also remember the officer on board our flagship told us that we had drifted approximately 40 miles. I do not think we will ever know exactly how far we drifted, but I do know that we survived regardless of how far we traveled. This same officer also told me that Wayne Neyland was picked up out of the water by a Japanese patrol boat and Elmer said that Wayne told him he actually made it all the way to the beach and swam up on shore. There are definitely some differences in our memory of our experience, but the important thing is that it is now a memory as opposed to a reality.

Elmer also said that Hobart and 'Doc' Eaves were buried at sea at 10:30 a.m. on September 18th about fifteen miles off the coast of Okinawa. They were the two that were tied together and found the next day along with George Wade. It was sad to know they were gone, but it was at least a little comforting to know that they were found and given a proper burial.

I never knew what island it was that we could see off in the distance before we were picked up and I always wondered what island it was. Well, in 1995, fifty years after our rescue, I was shown a photograph of Ie Shima from an Air Force buddy of mine named Bud Noggle who was on that island at the end of the war. When he showed me the photo he said, "Does this look familiar?" He said it was the island that war correspondent Ernie Pyle was killed on. I took that picture and I starred at it for the longest time because it sure looked just like the hill that I was starring at when I started thinking about the concept of faith. Bud told me that he knew that was the hill I could see off in the distance because it was the only island around Okinawa that had a hill with a peak on it. The rest of them were mostly flat. It turns out that Ie Shima was very far from where we were drifting and that some of the lower lying islands were much closer than we thought they were, but we could not see them because they were so low. If we were able to see them we might have actually been able to make it to one of them, but that never happened.

There was another minesweeper that sank the same night ours did, YMS – 421. However, they were in Buckner Bay when they went down. Eight sailors were killed and the rest survived. Apparently their ship was literally torn apart by the giant waves while it was in the bay.

Our typhoon was eventually named Makurazaki, but when it was developing out over the south pacific it had a different name. It actually started off with the name "Ida." Now that is irony. Looking back, I really wished it were my wife Ida and not the typhoon. She would have treated us more kindly.

Elmer was in the hospital on Okinawa Island when the second typhoon hit on October 12, 1945. He did not have to endure the torture of having to think it was going to happen again like we did. It was also quite a disappointment for Freeman being that it was his birthday. For his birthday present he was supposed to be sent home. Instead, he was placed back into one of those earth bound, real life nightmares that we honestly thought was going to toss us back into the sea and try to kill us again. But, we made it.

I was curious about the second typhoon so I did a little research. I found out that the name of it was "Louise." It was first seen developing on October 2nd in the Caroline Island chain. It went north and slowed a little and intensified as it passed over Okinawa. The winds were reported to be in excess of 90 miles per hour. It was said to be not as strong as ours, but it did sink 12 ships. A total of nine ships were sunk in our typhoon. It grounded 222 ships with 32 of them severely damaged. On Okinawa Island 36 people were confirmed dead and 47 were reported missing while 100 were seriously injured. Eighty-percent of the buildings in Buckner Bay were completely wiped out. All 60 airplanes on the island were damaged, but repairable and 107 amphibious craft were grounded and damaged. The amphibious craft were there in preparation for "Operation Olympic." This was the code name for the initial invasion of Japan that was scheduled for November 1, 1945. It was to begin on the island of Kyushu. By the time the typhoon "Louise" reached Japan, it was reduced to a tropical storm. Even though our nerves were more frayed in the second typhoon than in the first, I was just grateful we made it through a second one.

As the years passed I would frequently have memories of the experience come trickling into my head. There were so many factors that took place through the entire ordeal. We did not have the technology back then that we have today, so we had to rely on information over the radio from other ships or airplanes with regards to weather. We did not get a warning that the typhoon was coming until it was practically on top of us. When we did get the warning our Evaporator Water Conversion Unit, which was used to convert seawater into drinking water, was in pieces and being repaired on the deck of the ship.

We did not leave right away. We left about forty-five minutes after everybody else did because we put the evaporator unit back together. Our sister ship, the YMS – 454 left when the initial warning came in and she survived the typhoon unscathed. I often wondered what would have happened had we been given the warning an hour earlier. We would have had time to put the evaporator unit back together and be in the same position as the YMS – 454. Also, since we were not given the luxury of a distant early warning, I wonder what would have happened had we not spent the time putting the evaporator unit back together. Would we have been okay then? - Like the YMS – 454. There is no way we will ever know that. The only thing we do know is that, for the most part, the YMS – 472 was dealt a loosing hand with six points of light, the six men that survived. For a while there I was beating myself up with the "What if's." I had to stop doing that to myself because the guilt I was beginning to feel from it was taking its toll on me. It just did not seem fair that I was still here and the majority of my shipmates, who I spent time with on that ship since it was christened, were not here as well. There should have been something the military could have done to prevent such a horrible tragedy. But, the reality was always right there, what happened happened, and that is the way it is.

The other thing that went through my head for quite a while began when I made it home and Ida showed me a letter written by Wayne Neyland's mother. The letter basically said thank you to Ida for me, her husband, giving her son my life vest and sacrificing myself so that her son could live a full life. That letter really bothered me because I did not give him that life vest to sacrifice myself so that he could live. When he first asked for my vest I was very reluctant to give it up due to the fact that I kept it dry because the raft was getting a little lower in the water every day. I gave him that vest because he said he was going to swim and try to make it to the island we could see and get some help for all of us. According to the officer on the Flagship, a Japanese patrol boat picked up Wayne two or three hours after he left the raft. When they pulled him out of the water he never said a word about the other seven of us that were still on the raft. He just boarded, drank some water and was rescued. If he had told them we were still out there, we could not have been more than twenty or thirty minutes away if they decided to come look for us. After all, their ship did have a motor. They would have been there in time to prevent the deaths of Mendello, Plumb and Cullanan. I was really bothered by this concept. When Wayne's mother wrote that letter she had no idea that I had survived. Nor did Wayne. That would mean that Wayne told his mother the seven of us left on the raft did not make it. I was only left to conclude that Wayne wanted to be the only survivor of the ship. For some reason it must have seemed glorious to him to be the sole survivor.

His personality was such that he always wanted to be the center of attention while he was on board the ship, so the concept fit his personality like a glove. This was a tough pill to swallow, but I had no choice. It was forced down my throat. All I could do was remember that God was in control. Everything happens for a reason and I had to keep the faith. However, it was without a doubt, the epitome of self-centeredness. It was also the most selfish act I had ever seen anybody practice in my whole life and I can not believe that any sailor any where would ever do that to any of his shipmates.

It made it that much more difficult on me when I arrived home and Ida showed me a Western Union telegram dated October 18. It read; "GLAD BILL SURVIVED SEND ME ALL KNOWN DETAILS ON 472 COLLECT BY WIRE OR PHONE. HELEN M. PLUMB." This was Norman Plumb's wife. Had Wayne sent the patrol boat out to us, Norman Plumb probably would have survived. They had a daughter that would have been around a year old. In fact, I went on leave with Norman to Terryville, Connecticut when his daughter was born. He only met his daughter a very few times before we were shipped out to the Pacific. When I came home Ida showed me the telegram, so I called Helen and gave her the details of what happened. It was quite the difficult conversation because she was absolutely heartbroken and she just bawled her eyes out over the telephone. It was the toughest phone call I ever had to make in my life. She congratulated me on surviving, but there is really very little anybody can do under these types of circumstances. All one can do is keep the faith and let time do its healing.

Twenty some years later Norman's daughter came out to Whittier to visit Ida and myself. I do not know exactly how old she was at the time, but she was definitely in her early twenties. When I spoke with her I gave her the details of our six-day ordeal and how her father went under the water to get some pineapple juice when he thought he saw the ship below us, and how he never resurfaced. I explained to her the torment and pain I went through when I realized he was not coming back. She listened intently because she was so curious to learn the details of her father's fate. She did not cry because she said she had no memory of her father. She was maybe a year old when we sank, but she was still Norman Plumb's daughter and had an innate need to know the truth from the person he shared his last moments on this earth with. I made sure to be as honest with her as I possibly could. I also told her the miracle of our rescue and how true faith played such a vital role in me coming home and being able to tell her exactly what happened to her father. I told her it is always a good thing to keep God in your life and allow his ways to direct your choices and ultimately your life. After our talk, she told me that her mother remarried and still lived in Connecticut on a large farm with her new husband.

Over the years I did experience the feeling of guilt for being one of the survivors. At times I would feel it come in and try to overtake me, but I would not let it. I have to say that one of the best forms of therapy I have ever used was sharing my story and talking about all the details of it. It just seemed the more I spoke of the details and shared them with whomever was interested in listening the easier it was to live with it every day. Eventually there was no more guilt. For some reason, expressing my story over the years turned out to be pretty good medicine for myself. I also know that my relationship with God had much to do with my mental state. Just from my experience, I would have to say there has been no better remedy than telling the truth in detail whenever possible and allowing God to direct my path. It is a definite path to success. Not necessarily material success, but spiritual, mental and emotional success. And, when our life is functioning under that type of success, there really is nothing more we need except for food, water, shelter and family. When all of these are in place, we are a success.

I was so very fortunate to learn that God was in control of my life, and as I approach my 85th birthday, I have so much to be thankful for. I had a very loving and dear wife of 64 years before God decided it was time for her to go home to heaven. I thank God for my Christian heritage, as well as my mother, my father, my family and my whole congregation. They never stopped praying for my rescue. I was grateful to Coast Savings and Loans for helping me keep the promise I made to God while I was floating aimlessly on the raft. Because of them I was able to speak to literally thousands of people and share the miracle of the rescue to people who were not even sure what true faith was. I often think back to the day we were rescued. It was about forty-five minutes before sunset when those three Corsairs went flying across the sky. They had to be at least seven or eight miles away from us, as well as flying parallel to us. I remember seeing the last plane in the formation make a left turn and start heading in our direction while the other two planes kept going straight. There was no way he should have been able to see us from that far away. The raft was a grayish blue color as were the clothes we were wearing. The only thing that was a contrast to the blue ocean water was the white T-shirt I was waiving in the air. But, for some reason he headed directly for us as if he could see right where we were. And, like I said, when that plane dipped its left wing and began circling us I knew beyond a shadow of a doubt it was true faith being answered. I always wanted to talk to the pilot of that third plane. I wanted to ask him why he turned when he turned and why he turned where he turned. Did he actually see us? Did he see something that peaked his curiosity? Did he have an intuition? Did something just tell him to make that turn when he did? Or, was he just goofing around and trying to fly away from his buddies? Those were questions that I was never able to find the answer to. The strange thing about these three Corsairs was that when I did some further research, there was no record of any Corsairs in the area at that time. When Elmer Renner was doing the research for his book he also found no record of these Corsairs in the area. He checked military records and they just kept telling him that there were no Corsairs in that area on that date. Well, obviously there were or I would not be here telling my story. I think things were just a little unorganized due to the end of the war and the discharge of so many military personal that it would be very easy to not know if there were three Corsairs in the area. Regardless of all that, I was never given the chance to thank that pilot that turned his plane in our direction. However, I think that he was satisfied enough to know that he was the one that spotted four lost and drifting sailors somewhere in the Pacific Ocean. He probably had no idea how close to death we were, but that did not matter. We were rescued and we were all going home. As for my shipmates who never made it home, there has not been a day goes by that I have not thought of them since September 16, 1945. And, as I said earlier, for every church I built, two-by-four nailed down and brick cemented into place, I did so with them in mind. And for every word written, comma placed, period dotted, capital checked and sentence structured I do so again in memory of them, and in dedication to them.

None of us should ever forget that God is a good God, and when God says he will answer our prayers, then he *will* answer our prayers. But first, we need to understand what true prayer is. True prayer is one hundred percent selfless and directed toward those who need it the most. If we ask God to bring us gifts of materialism for our own selfish desires, it probably will not happen. But, if we have given our all, and there is nothing else we can do and we ask God to feed us when we are hungry and when we have no food, he will always answer our prayers.

Acknowledgements

A book is never complete without a "Thank You!" list, so a thank you goes out to Randy Twycross for allowing me to leave work at busy times and go out and tell my story, Freeman Hetzer for sharing his memories of our ordeal, Ida Mae Harrison for her endless love and support and 63 years of wonderful marriage, Elmer Renner for his statistical information, Forrest Haggerty for bringing my story to life in book form, Dr. John Harsany Jr. for his endless support and always being on the ready when needed, my dear and wonderful family members for their perpetual unconditional love and support, the group of ladies who edited the book, Shirley Berkner, Naz Kassamali, Janice Urick, Ave Brown, Candace Harsany, Louise McDonald, Marge Lord, Joanne Smith, and last, but definitely not least, I would like to thank God for my Christian heritage, the miracle of my rescue and the chance to share that miracle to many people through my lectures and now in book form. If by chance I happened to not remember somebody I would like to say thank you and please know that you are truly not forgotten.

Herbert Ralph "Bill" Harrison. This photo was taken during his basic training in San Diego, California.

Bill's wife Ida Mae Harrison working in a factory and doing her part for the war effort.

Bill, Ida and Richie in Miami, Florida.

– Bill's fire unit in Miami, Florida. Bill is standing in the front row second from the left.

Bill's childhood friend Sammy Cooper sitting on the left. His two nephews Ovie Broussard sitting in the middle and Benny Broussard sitting on the right, their dog "Pooch," and Bill standing with his football under his arm.

YMS – 472.

The rectangular life raft can be seen mounted on the side of the ship.

Having fun on deck, from left to right, John Roy Eaves Jr., Stanley Zacharus Marks and Lt. Boyd Weaver Stauffer.

Edward Cecil Hicks, the Yeoman that told Bill he was too sick to stay in the wheelhouse. He was never seen again.

Donald Raymond Hartman, Bill's shipmate who was killed by the sharks.

Joseph Robert Quather, he went down with the ship and was never seen again.

From left to right, Norman Wolcott Plumb, Bill Harrison and John Roy Eaves Jr. After thinking he saw the ship below the raft, Norman Plumb swam down to get some pineapple juice and never returned.

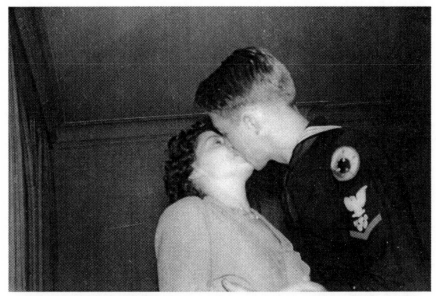

Norman Plumb kissing his wife Helen. The two had an infant daughter at this time.

Donald Clyde Van Arman on the left and Freeman Theodore Hetzer on the right. Van Arman was the sailor attempting to signal for help with a lantern as the ship was sinking.

Norman Plumb, left, and Bill Harrison, right, on liberty.

Joseph Francis Mendello. After drinking too much seawater and frantically
swimming away from the raft, he was never seen again.

Elmer John Renner on the left and Lt. Boyd Weaver Stauffer on the right. Lt. Stauffer went down with the ship.

Charles Eurcel Sigfriet. While anchored in New Port Beach, California, Sifgriet's wife came down from Eugene, Oregon and stayed at Bill's house with Charles for a month. She was pregnant with their first child. Charles was never seen again after the typhoon and he never had the chance to meet his first child.

Stanley Zacharus Marks. After the typhoon he was never seen again.

Charles Griffith Bates Jr. went down with the ship and was never seen again.

Thomas William Boivin went down with the ship and was never seen again.

Some of the YMS – 472 crewmembers during chow time.

YMS – 472 crewmembers during chow time.

From left to right, Richard Edmond Lewis, Donald Raymond Hartman, Charles Griffith Bates Jr., and Paul Joseph Termine Jr. These are four shipmates who never made it home.

John Roy Eaves Jr. on the left and Robert Hobart on the right. Their lifeless bodies were pulled from the water the next day with their life vests tied together.

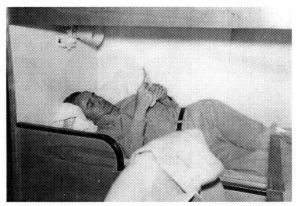

Lt. Boyd Weaver Stauffer. He was never seen again after the typhoon.

Paul Joseph Termine Jr. He was never seen again after the typhoon.

Paul Termine and Donald Hartman taking a break.

Paul Termine, Richard Emond Lewis, Stanley Marks and Thomas William Boivin.
All four sailors perished the night of the typhoon.

Donald Van Arman. He was never seen again after the typhoon.

Elmer Renner on the left, and Bill Harrison on the right during a brief shore leave in San Diego, California. This was the YMS – 472's first stop in the United States after passing through the Panama Canal.

WESTERN UNION

The filing time shown in the date line on telegrams and day letters is STANDARD TIME at point of origin. Time of receipt is STANDARD TIME at point of destination.

SY 46 GOVT

WASHINGTON DC 641pm Sept 26-45

MRS IDA G MAE HARRISON

211 RICHMOND DR PICO CALIF

I DEEPLY REGRET TO INFORM YOU THAT YOUR HUSBAND HERBERT RALPH
HARRISON FIREMAN FIRST CLASS USRN IS MISSING AS RESULT OF A
TYPHOON ON 16 SEPT 1945 IN THE SERVICE OF HIS COUNTRY YOUR GREAT
ANXIETY IS APPRECIATED AND YOU WILL BE FURNISHED DETAILS WHEN
RECEIVED.

VICE ADMIRAL LEWIS BENFELD THE CHIEF OF NAVAL PERSONNEL

541pm

This was the first telegram that Ida received four days after Bill's rescue.

In reply address not the signer of this
letter, but Bureau of Naval Personnel,
Navy Department, Washington 25, D.C.

Refer to No.

Pers-53230-mtk
564 09 45

NAVY DEPARTMENT
BUREAU OF NAVAL PERSONNEL
WASHINGTON 25, D. C.

28 September 1945

Mrs. Ida Mae Harrison
211 Richmond Drive
Pico, California

Dear Mrs. Harrison:

It is with regret that this Bureau confirms the report that
your husband, Herbert Ralph Harrison, Motor Machinist's Mate
second class, United States Naval Reserve, is being carried
on the official records in the status of missing.

Details in connection with your husband's disappearance have
not been received. However, because of the intensive search
which is being carried out in all areas at the present time,
information clarifying the status of missing personnel is
being received daily. It is hoped that a report will be
received concerning your husband in the near future.

Sincere sympathy is extended to you in your anxiety. You are
assured that any further information received will be forwarded
to you promptly.

You are urged to read the enclosed booklet carefully as it
explains matters of importance concerning naval personnel in
the missing status.

By direction of Chief of Naval Personnel.

Sincerely yours,

H. E. ATKINSON
Commander, USNR.
Officer in Charge
Casualty Section

Encl.

This was the Naval letter that came a few days after the first Western Union
Telegram came.

CLASS OF SERVICE

This is a full-rate Telegram or Cable-gram unless its de-ferred character is in-dicated by a suitable symbol above or pre-ceding the address.

WESTERN UNION

A. N. WILLIAMS
PRESIDENT

SYMBOLS

DL = Day Letter

NT = Overnight Telegram

LC = Deferred Cable

NLT = Cable Night Letter

Ship Radiogram

The filing time shown in the date line on telegrams and day letters is STANDARD TIME at point of origin. Time of receipt is STANDARD TIME at point of destination

SY 68 GOVT

WASHINGTON DC 724pm Oct 4-45

MRS IDA MAE HARRISON

211 RICHMOND DR PICO CALIF

I AM PLEASED TO INFORM YOU THAT YOUR HUSBAND HERBERT RALPH HARRISON MOTOR MACHINISTS MATE SECOND CLASS USNR PREVIOUSLY REPORTED MISSING AS RESULT OF TYPHOON 16 SEPTEMBER 1945 WHILE IN THE SERVICE OF HIS COUNTRY IS NOW REPORTED TO BE A SUVIVOR. UNDOUBTEDLY HE WILL COMMUNICATE WITH YOU AT AN EARLY DATE CONCERNING HIS WELFARE AND WHEREABOUTS. THE XXXXXXXX ANXIETY CAUSED YOU BY THE PREVIOUS MESSAGE IS DEEPLY REGRETTED.

VICE ADMIRAL LOUIS DENFELD THE CHIEF OF NAVAL
PERSONNEL

555pm

THE COMPANY WILL APPRECIATE SUGGESTIONS FROM ITS PATRONS CONCERNING ITS SERVICE

This was the second telegram Ida received ten days after Bill's rescue.

CLASS OF SERVICE

This is a full-rate Telegram or Cable-gram unless its de-ferred character is in-dicated by a suitable symbol above or pre-ceding the address.

WESTERN UNION

A. N. WILLIAMS
PRESIDENT

SYMBOLS

DL = Day Letter

NL = Night Letter

LC = Deferred Cable

NLT = Cable Night Letter

Ship Radiogram

The filing time shown in the date line on telegrams and day letters is STANDARD TIME at point of origin. Time of receipt is STANDARD TIME at point of destination

S49 15=HARTFORD CONN OCT 18 100P

MRS HERBERT R HARRISON=

530 MAGNOLIA AVE WH=

GLAD BILL SURVIVED SEND ME ALL KNOW DETAILS ON 472 COLLECT BY WIRE OR PHONE=

HELEM M PLUMB.

(11)

472.

This was the telegram that Ida received from Norman Plumb's wife nearly one month after the ordeal.

Our Servicemen Write—

Not Missing in Action

Mrs. B. J. Harrison of Whittier, California, received a telegram from the army that her son Bill was missing in action after his ship was sunk on September 16. She felt that God had promised her son would be spared, so in spite of the telegram she held fast to the promise. Sometime later she received a letter from her son written on September 23 which told of his experiences after his ship was sunk. The following lines are taken from this letter.

"I am still a little weak, but I will try to get a few lines off to you. After our ship sank, nine of us drifted on a raft that had no bottom. We paddled with our hands for five days. During those five days, five of the boys died, for we had no food or water. Each day I would remind the boys to pray, and they were more than willing. I told them that I had a praying mother and father and wife and knew that if we would hold on and keep the faith that God would see us through. We were picked up late one evening and now the remaining four of us are on a hospital ship in Okinawa.

"I am okay, Mom, and my life belongs to God. I made Him that promise while I was out there on the raft. Sometimes it would seem as though there was no hope of being found, but I would remember my wife and little son and I would say to myself, 'I must get back.' I hope to see you soon."—H. R. Harrison

This interview of Bill's mother came out in a local paper in Whittier, California after Bill's rescue.

Bill on board the YMS – 472.

The four Harrison boys. The two in back, from left to right, Luke and Claude.
The two in front, from left to right, Royce "Red" and Bill.

The entire Harrison clan. Back row from left to right, Claude, Royce "Red,"
Helen, Bill and Luke. Front row from left to right, Floy, Ima Fay, Zella (mom),
Jack (Dad), Cassie and Jimmie.

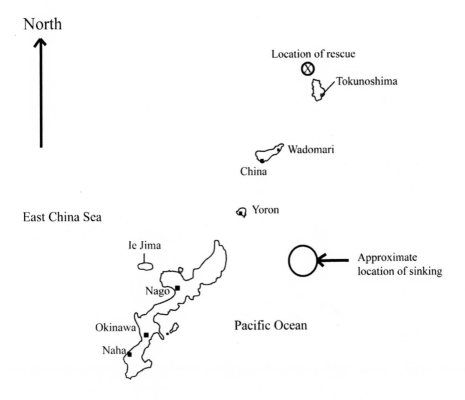

This map shows the approximate location of the YMS – 472's sinking, and the location of where the remaining four were picked up. They drifted 60 to 70 miles north before they were finally rescued on the sixth day.

LaVergne, TN USA
08 November 2009
163366LV00002B/2/A